REMEMBERING

WARTIME

Ascot Sunningdale and

Sunninghill

1939 - 1945

GW00673411

Christine Weightman

This book is dedicated to all those who remembered

With much love from Peggy and Arthur

Published by Cheapside Publications
Heronsbrook Cottage · Ascot · SL5 7QG
Printed and bound in Great Britain by Anthony Rowe
of Chippenham and Reading

CONTENTS

All prices are given in old pounds, shillings and pence. For those too young to remember this currency: £1 equals 20 shillings (s) or 240 pennies (d); 1s equals 12d; a half crown equals 2s 6d i.e. twelve and a half new pence; a tanner equals 6d; 1d equals less than half a new pence.

ILLUSTRATIONS AND MAPS

Finding appropriate local photographs was difficult. Film was hard to obtain during the war and photographs of military sites and of bomb damaged buildings were forbidden unless taken by official photographers. I have therefore used some photographs taken before or after the war. Where individuals have been identified on the group photographs they are named. It would be very interesting to hear from anyone who can identify others.

I am very grateful to John End and Trevor Lewis who made their large collections of photographs and postcards available and to all others who generously lent photographs and made maps. They are attributed as follows: J.C. is Joyce Cook, J.E. is John End, G.G. is Grace Gill, V.H. is Vera Hathaway, I.K. is Irv Kirsh, T.L. is Trevor Lewis, IWM is Imperial War Museum; S.P. is Stella de St Paer, E.R. is Enid Reeves, C.S. is Cyril Smith, M.W. is Mary Wood, S.W. is Sheila Williams, J.W. is John Weightman

SOURCES

Archives:

Berkshire Record Office

Ascot Heath Girls School Minute Book, D/P185 28-31; C/El 109/1-4.

Friends of Euryalus D/EX 1043/1; Parish Magazines and PC Minutes for St Michael's, Sunninghill, All Souls, South Ascot and All Saints, Ascot: D/P 126, 185 and 186; WRDC Council Minutes: RD/WI Ca 1/22-27; WRDC Committees: RD/WI Cb 1/1; WRDC Rate Books: RD/WI/FR/3/5-6; WRDC Sewerage: RD/WI cc 3-4

British Library, the Newspaper Archive

The Windsor Slough and Eton Express 1939-1946

Durning Library Ascot, Local History Collection

Imperial War Museum

Memoir of Winifred Lane; Merriman Papers; Wiseman Papers

Public Record Office Kew

Ascot Camp No 7: HO 214, 215/52, 283/1-4, 144/22454 21247; 215/52; CRES 35/1408; FO 939/E377, 939/339, 939/342, 939/426; Agriculture: MAF 169/51, WO 32/16666; Education: ED: 32/118, 638; 138/8

Secondary sources:

The A.A. Handbook 1937-38

Bill Bates & Les Parry, *"The Fascinating History of Ascot Ex-Service Men's Club"*, 1999

William Boddy, *"The History of Brooklands 1906-1940"*, London, 1957

Isla Brownless, *"Lambrook in Wartime"*, 1995

Angus Calder, *"The People's War Britain 1939-1945"*, London, 1969

John Charnley, *"Blackshirts and Roses"*, 1990

Harold Clunn, *"The Face of the Home Counties"*, 1936

S. M. Ferguson and H. Fitzgerald, *"History of the Second World War. Studies in the Social Services"*, HMSO, 1954

Juliet Gardiner, *"Wartime Britain 1939-1945"*, London 2004

Percy Hathaway, *"Some Ramblings of an Old Bogonian"*, 1995

Norman Longmate, *"How We Lived Then"*, London, 2002

H. R. Madol, *"The League of London"*, London, 1942

Sean Magee and Sally Aird, *"Ascot the History"*, 2002

Clifford Smith *"The Great Park Windsor Forest"*, 2004

Sheila Stewart, *"A Home from Home"*, Longmans 1967

Jonathan Riley Smith, *"The Franciscans and the Parish of Ascot 1887-1980"*

Jane Roberts, *"Royal Landscape The Gardens and Parks of Windsor"*, 1999

E. Varley edited by Wendy James, *"The Judy Story the dog with six lives"*, 1973.

PREFACE

This account is based on a series of interviews with people who lived in Ascot, Sunninghill and Sunningdale during the war. While the older men and women were more aware of the whole picture, some of the best evidence came from young boys who somehow always managed to be where they were not supposed to be. They had often been eyewitnesses to events shrouded in wartime secrecy and red tape. Everyone had a tale to tell. Daily life and special events were all recalled with a remarkable clarity that bore witness to the powerful impact of the wartime experience. When a story came from just one person it is attributed but when several told the same story there is no attribution.

I am very grateful to all the following who shared their memories with me: Mavis Bagshaw, Martie Brett, Gordon Butcher, Peggy and Arthur Clark, Mavis Colman, Joyce Cook, Ian Cooper, Vernon Cox, Florence End, John End, Margaret Finlay, David Franklin, Aprilla Gilfrin, Grace Gill, Mary Grove, Vera and Percy Hathaway, Jerry Jerome, Irene Jones, George Laney, Mary and Trevor Lewis, Irv Kirch, John Mason, Bert Melhuish, Peter Pack, Albert Page, Natalie Paknadel, Elsie Phillips, Eric Reed, Enid Reeves, Louis Russell, Graham Salter, Hazel Sharman, Paul Snook, Laura Sparks, Adrian Turner, John Wigmore, Mary Wood, Doris Woodbine, Roma Young and Robert Zerilli.

Interviews were followed by research at the Berkshire Record Office, the Public Record Office, the Durning Local History Archive at the Ascot Library, the British Library Press Archive at Colindale and the Imperial War Museum. I was particularly grateful to be able to use John End's private collection of documents relating to the history of this area. Thanks are also due to: Joan Cooper who allowed me to use and publish her late husband Philip Cooper's work on the War Memorials at All Saints in Ascot, All Souls in South Ascot and St Michael's in Sunninghill; Dorothy Davis of the Egham History Society who gave me useful advice on the Surrey area; Professor Martin Parsons of the Research Centre for Evacuees and War Child Studies at the University of Reading for his advice; Stella de St Paer who allowed me to use some of her war-telegrams and air-telegraphs; Jackie Wilson, the headmistress, who let me read the Log Books of St Francis' School in South Ascot; Sheila Williams who advised me on knitting and lent me the booklet *"Knitting for the Army"*; Sister Camilla Walkin of the Marist Convent who provided information about Eisenhower at Frogmore.

Gordon Butcher, John End, Percy Hathaway and Trevor Lewis helped by reading through the manuscript. Any errors that remain are my responsibility.

Ascot, Sunningdale and Sunninghill 1939 – 1945

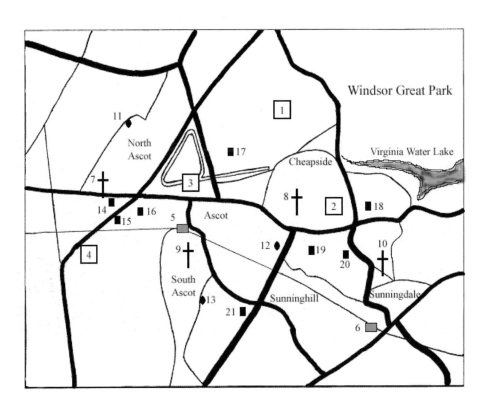

Camps

USAAF at Sunninghill Park	1
Silwood Park	2
Ascot Race Course	3
Internment Camp No 7	4

Railway Stations

Ascot	5
Sunningdale	6

Churches

All Saints, Ascot	7
St Michael's, Sunninghill	8
All Souls, South Ascot	9
Holy Trinity, Sunningdale	10

Schools

Ascot Heath	11
Sunninghill School	12
St Francis'	13

Other Buildings

Englemere Wood	14
Englemere	15
Heatherwood Hospital	16
Ascot Farm	17
Little Paddocks	18
Frognal	19
Sunningdale Park	20
Berystede Hotel	21

FROM PEACE TO WAR

Ascot High Street in the 1930s

On the Eve of War

"A beautiful district on the fringe of Windsor Great Park ... famed for its golf courses, the presence of the Prince of Wales' estate at Fort Belvedere and the Ascot Racecourse". This according to Harold Clunn was a fair description of our area in 1936 with Ascot itself a *"modern and very select village"*. Compared to the present day it was indeed *"select"* and also a very rural *"village"*.

It was nevertheless a busy and bustling place. There were several hotels to accommodate race goers and tourists. All the villages and even hamlets like Cheapside in Sunninghill had their own post offices and two or three inns. Each district had a variety of shops, with drapers, general stores, garages, bicycle and camera shops in Ascot and Sunninghill. Sunningdale, the smallest of the three villages, was a good example of the generous provision of shops in the pre-war era with three grocers' shops as well as a butcher's, fishmonger's, sweetshop and tobacconist's. In Upper Village Road Sunninghill, there were no less than five grocers and there were others close by in the High Street.

1

Most homes were thus within easy walking distance of shops and this was a great asset.

Sunningdale High Street in the 1940s

Even if a shop was some distance away it was no problem for the housewife since almost all tradesmen made regular deliveries to their customers. The grocers' and butchers' boys would call to collect orders and then return with the goods. Bakers went the rounds two or three times a week carrying a choice of bread right up to the doorstep. Much of this delivery service continued during the war.

Most local men were employed close to home as general labourers, gardeners or woodmen. There was a small permanent labour force at the Ascot Racecourse and in the hotels and inns. During Race Week, these workers were supplemented by an army of extra helpers recruited locally. The largest employer was the Ascot and District Gas and Electricity Company, known as the Sunninghill Gasworks or the Town Gas. In Sunningdale there was also a joinery works, Fassnidge, Son and Norris, near the Station Parade. When this was destroyed by a fire in February 1943 forty men and women lost their jobs. There were several sawmills and builder's yards and at least two blacksmiths in Sunninghill. These forges were still working long after the war was over, one until 1954 and the last blacksmith's, Morton's (on the London Road about 200 yards from Silwood Corner) closed in the 1960s. Changes however were already on the way. By 1939 some men were already commuting to

London. This traffic increased dramatically during the war when workmen's trains left Ascot and Sunningdale every morning to help to clear up after air raids.

The Sunninghill Gas Works in the 1920s

Local women had little choice of employment. They usually went from school into domestic service until they married and had children. Thereafter they stayed at home, returning to domestic service, shop or laundry work when they could and if they needed to. The war would bring far more opportunities.

In 1939 there were less than 2,000 residential properties in the whole of Ascot, Sunningdale and Sunninghill. The total population was under 8,000 (28,078 in 2001). Almost all of these villages was administered by the Windsor Rural District Council (hereafter WRDC). There were two exceptions. Old Sunningdale lay in Berkshire but those parts of Sunningdale along the A30 such as Shrubs Hill and the Sunningdale railway station were in Surrey. Old Sunningdale was the heart of the village with the main church, schools, shops and most of the houses. Similarly parts of North Ascot lay within the administration of Winkfield Parish. Children from the centre of Ascot attended Ascot Heath School in Fernbank Road, also in Winkfield.

This corner of Berkshire was known for its mixture of very large estates with scattered clusters of small rented houses and cottages. Mains drainage, gas and electricity had all been made available in the

1930s but many of the cottages were without these services. There were still many outdoor privies, some emptied into weekly carts, others into a midden by their owners and *"producing very good vegetables"*. Many families had no electricity, gas or hot water. One cold tap downstairs, paraffin lamps and candles were the norm and meals were cooked over the fire or on the range beside it. The WRDC had agreed plans to install electricity in all their council houses but the work stopped in 1940 due to the shortage of men and materials.

All the larger houses had gas and electricity supplies, mains water and modern sanitation, sometimes to cesspits. Their owners were public servants, bankers, servicemen or businessmen, many of whom were retired. Their wives would never work outside the home and hardly within it since they were very well supplied with a number of servants. When war came some of the largest estates were requisitioned and rarely returned to private ownership. Other families made room for refugees and evacuees or moved out to provide space for evacuated schools and children's homes.

Sunningdale Park in the 1950s

Most of the domestic servants, household staff and almost all the gardeners and gamekeepers went off into the services or to war work. Only the elderly and infirm were left to manage these large properties. As a result many of the larger houses were closed down or requisitioned. Very few of the bigger estates stayed in private hands throughout the war. There were however some families like the Fullarton James' at

Beech Grove, the Turle's at The Cedars, Ascot, and the Cunliffe Owen's at Sunningdale Park who managed to retain their housekeepers, cooks and some of their maids. Even when the families remained in residence, the great lawns, grass tennis courts and parterres were dug up to grow potatoes and the swimming pools were emptied. Everyone was expected to do *"their bit for the war effort".*

The Crest of the WRDC

September the Third 1939

At eleven fifteen on the morning of Sunday, the third of September, Roma Browning, a twelve year old, was sitting quietly listening to the wireless with her grandparents who had a greengrocery in South Ascot. The Prime Minister Mr Chamberlain declared that we were now at war with Germany. Roma remembers being very frightened by the announcement. Her mother was dead and her father was away at sea with the Naval Reserve. Aprilla Gilfrin, who was eighteen, also sat at home with her parents to listen to the Prime Minister's speech. When it was over she looked at the expressions on her parents' faces and walked out leaving them alone with each other.

Many people were still away on their summer holidays. Mary Wood was at Southsea with her parents. Her father had been a soldier in the *"War to end all Wars"* and they were staying with her aunt who had also served as a nurse. Mary remembers that they stood together in silence on the front and watched as soldiers were already embarking in the harbour. Her father commented sadly *"many would go and many would not return"*. They then hurried home to Ascot.

Gordon Butcher had come home early from his holiday arriving in Ascot on the Friday because his Aunt Mabel, along with all the other London teachers, had been ordered to return to her school in London to prepare for the evacuation. On the way back from Dorset they saw trucks full of troops heading for the south coast and they all realised that war was very close indeed. Gordon heard about the declaration of war when he was at Mrs Brady's house in New Road, stuffing straw palliasses to make beds for the many evacuees who had already begun to arrive. When the Reverend H. A. Walton, Rector of All Saints Church, drove past, he stopped his car to scold them for missing church.

Sheila Stewart, an evacuee, who had arrived at Englemere Wood, did not miss church. She had heard the Reverend Walton announce that war was declared and call for two minutes silence followed by prayers for the country and the armed forces.

All Saints Church Ascot

St Alban's Church Windlesham

Trevor Lewis was a choirboy at another nearby church, St Albans, Windlesham (now vanished, this church was on the south side of the A30 at Sunningdale almost opposite to the entrance to Devenish Road). He remembers *"the vicar looking very stern and going into the pulpit at the start of the morning service and saying, 'Please sit down. I have a serious announcement to make with the authority of the bishop'. He then read out the official statement from the Prime Minister ... and we were at war."*

John Wigmore was only seven years old. He was told that we were at war when he was out playing with his mates. Terrified he rushed back home to his mother who reassured him, promising him that, *"the Germans aren't coming today".*

Irene Jones was a young mother visiting her parents when she heard that war had been declared. She was immediately alarmed being all too aware that her husband and her four brothers would be called up. All fortunately survived the war though her youngest brother was left with permanent injuries. Florence End and Mary Grove were both young women with their first babies and they too were horrified. Florence was alone in the house with her baby son when she heard the announcement. She went round to her mother-in-law's house where her husband had his photographic studio and they *"all worried together"*. She and her husband decided not to have any more children until times were safer. They reckoned that with only one baby you could always pick him up and run if you had to.

Mary Grove, her husband Roy and their three-month-old baby were in their new home in the High Street, Sunningdale, and she was busy cooking the lunch when they heard the news. She had good reason to be afraid knowing about her parents' experience in the First World War when her father had been wounded and gassed. He still had health problems from his injuries and from the frostbite he had endured. She had two brothers and feared for them and for her husband. Mary and Roy also felt that this was not a world to bring children into and they put off having a second child until well after the war.

From even a brief survey such as this it is evident that the reaction to the outbreak of war was very similar. Most people had been expecting the bad news. Mothers with young children remember being especially frightened. Those who had direct experience of the First World War were disappointed that war had not been avoided. But among the young men and the boys there were many who can now recall their excitement at the news and admit, ruefully, that they thought of it at the time as the start of a great adventure.

Off to War

Under the Military Training Bill of April 1939 all twenty-year old men had become liable for three and a half years training and service in the Territorial Army or the Naval and Air Force Reserves. As soon as war was declared the Territorial Army was merged with the Regular Army and all men between eighteen and forty-one became liable for conscription. By the end of September there were 897,000 men in the services. In 1941 the upper age was extended to fifty-one years and women were also included.

At the peak of war in May 1945 there would be an army of 2,920,000 men. This amounted to thirty percent of the male working population and over half of them were married. The absence of so many husbands, fathers, sons and brothers and daughters brought hardship for many and heartache for everyone. Very few local families were spared these personal dramas. In May 1940, Reverend Gerald Thursfield, the Vicar of St Michael's at Sunninghill, considered keeping a list in the church porch with the names of all the parishioners who were serving in the forces but it was decided that the list would be far too long and probably inaccurate as well.

Many local men served in the Royal Berkshire Regiment and some were present at the Regimental Review held in Bagshot Park by their

Commander in Chief, His Royal Highness the Duke of Connaught. On September 16th the first units departed with the Expeditionary Force for France and throughout that winter more and more men went overseas. Colin Turner left in January 1940 with the 3rd Battalion of the Royal Berkshires. He was a twenty-four year old post office engineer, married with three young children and living in Trinity Crescent. Although he was ill with influenza he wanted to travel with his mates. He died of meningitis soon after landing in France becoming the first Sunningdale man lost in the war. His brother was killed later in Italy.

The Royal Berkshires fought in Belgium and France and struggled back from La Panne and Dunkirk at the end of May. Six more local men lost their lives in this campaign. The youngest was Herbert *"Jumbo"* Lee, twenty years old. William Openshaw of Fernbank Road Ascot died in Belgium in the September of 1940 only four months after his younger nineteen year old brother Ernest had been killed on HMS Esk. Private Jack Waldron of Pond Cottage Queens Hill Ascot, near the Golden Gates Lodge, was taken prisoner. He was fortunate enough to be one of the few repatriated in 1943 during an exchange of prisoners. Even more perished in the Anzio battles of early 1944. Over a hundred Royal Berkshires men died and the Tenth Battalion was disbanded.

Although the losses were less than in the First World War, ninety-eight men and one woman are named on the War Memorials of the local parishes. They died serving in Burma and India, Egypt and North Africa, Italy, Greece, North Europe and at home.

1939 - 45 WAR

J. ACKLAND	R. TWISLETON	M. A. HAYFIELD	B. SHARPE
T. BINT	- WYKEHAM	A. HOPKINS	I. E. STAMPER
P. BINT	- FIENNES	P. W. KIMPTON	R. STAMPER
C. H. COBBE	A. E. GEORGE	J. A. MACKINTOSH	G. TAYLOR
A. J. CLARK	J. B. GORDON	A. W. PORTER	R. TAYLOR
F. G. CLARK	A. GROVE	E. REED	E. E. TEMPEST
H. L. CUNLIFFE	G. GROVE	D. W. REED	A. TURNER
- OWEN	R. A. HAIG	K. RIDEOUT	C. TURNER
	F. HALL	C. RUBY	J. A. UNDERWOOD
			R. N. WEIR

Sunningdale War Memorial

The War Memorials have a few omissions and three young men are named on two Memorials. One of these was William Perkins, he lived in South Ascot so is remembered at All Soul's but he was a leader of the boys club in Sunninghill and is also remembered at St Michael's. Marguerite Rance of Lower Village Road Sunninghill is the only woman commemorated. She died serving in the WRAF while operating a barrage balloon installation, a heavy and dangerous job. There were several deaths involving these installations.

Holy Trinity Church Sunningdale

The majority of those commemorated were in the Army but about twenty were in the RAF, including Douglas Weatherill of South Ascot who was awarded the Distinguished Flying Cross. Twelve died in the Royal Navy, including Hugo Cunliffe Owen from Sunningdale Park and at least five perished in the Merchant Marine. Their deaths were spread across all six years of the war peaking in 1945. The Sunningdale Memorial records the deaths of seven pairs of young men from the same families: T. and P. Bint, A. J. and F. G. Clark, A. and G. Grove, E. and D. W. Reed, I. F. and R. Stamper, G. and R. Taylor and C. and A. Turner.

The two Clark boys, who died aged eighteen and twenty, were both airmen. These charming young men are remembered by many people in Sunningdale including Grace Gill who had been their neighbour and childhood friend. The two Stamper brothers were also in the RAF and their father was the licensee of The Red Lion on the London Road. Eric

Reed still feels the loss of his two brothers who both died at the age of twenty-three. David Reed served as a corporal in the Royal Marine Commando and was, as Eric remembers sadly, *"the smartest soldier you ever saw, every button and badge gleaming"*. He was killed in action six days after D-Day. His brother Edward died later, serving with the Royal Engineers in Germany. The Reed family lived in Bedford Lane. Each of these losses affected many lives in these small communities.

John and Fred Clark of Sunningdale

Most local servicemen however were lucky enough to survive the whole war like Vera Hathaway's father who went to Egypt with the Eighth Army. There were some remarkable escapes such as eighteen-year old Donald Bourne of Shrubs Hill House, Sunningdale who came home after ten days adrift in the Arctic. There was great bravery too. In January 1941, Lieutenant Michael Tufnell RN was awarded a Distinguished Service Order for bravery in the defence of a convoy in the Channel and later his brother Tim was awarded the Military Cross.

At home anxiety was made worse by the frequent lack of communication. Keeping in touch was not easy. Many men were moved from place to place especially after the winter of 1943. There was also the problem of censorship. All military correspondence was censored and this would create long delays for letters. A popular way to keep in touch was via special war telegrams where number codes could be sent off quickly. A telegram was dispatched by selecting a series of numbers

CORRESPONDENCE

1. Letter received many thanks
2. Letters received many thanks
3. Telegram received many thanks
4. Parcel received many thanks
5. Parcels received many thanks
6. Letters and parcels received many thanks
7. Letter and telegram received many thanks
8. Telegram and parcels received many thanks
9. Letters sent
10. Parcels sent
11. Letters and parcels sent
12. Many thanks for letter
13. Many thanks for parcel
14. Many thanks for telegram
15. No news of you for some time
16. Writing
17. Urgent
18. Please write or telegraph
19. Please write
20. Please telegraph
21. Please reply worried

GREETINGS

26. Greetings
27. Loving greetings
28. Fondest greetings
29. Love
30. Darling
31. All my love
32. All my love dearest
33. All our love
34. Fondest love
35. Fondest love darling

36. Best wishes
37. Greetings from us all
38. Loving greetings from all of us
39. Best wishes from all of us
40. Fondest wishes from all of us
41. Best wishes and good health
42. Kisses
43. Love and kisses
44. Fondest love and kisses
45. Well
46. All well at home
47. Best wishes for Christmas
48. Best wishes for Christmas and New Year
49. Loving wishes for Christmas
50. Loving wishes for Christmas and New Year
51. Loving Christmas thoughts
52. Happy Christmas
53. Happy Christmas and New Year
54. Good luck
55. Keep smiling
56. My thoughts are with you
57. Many happy returns
58. Birthday greetings
59. Loving birthday greetings
60. Happy anniversary
61. You are more than ever in my thoughts at this time
62. Best wishes for a speedy return
63. Good show keep it up
64. Best wishes for New Year

HEALTH

68. Family all well
69. All well children evacuated
70. All well children returned home

71. All well and safe
72. Are you all right
73. Are you all right worried about you
74. Please don't worry
75. Hope you are improving
76. Please telegraph that you are well
77. Are you ill
78. Have you been ill
79. Illness is not serious
80. Illness is serious
81. I have left hospital
82. In bad health
83. Health improving
84. Health fully restored
85. Son born
86. Daughter born

PROMOTION

91. Congratulations on your promotion
92. Very pleased to hear of your promotion
93. Delighted hear about your promotion

MONEY

98. Please send me £X
99. Please send me $X
100. Have sent you £X
101. Have sent you $X

Note.—The actual amount in words to be inserted immediately after the text number.

102. Can you send me any money
103. Glad if you could send some money
104. Have received money
105. Have you received money
106. Have you sent money
107. Thanks for money received

Texts for Telegrams

such as 74, 32, 56, which would be decoded and delivered as *"Please don't worry, All my love dearest, My thoughts are with you"*. Keen letter writers might use airgraphs, minute letter forms about 4 by 5 inches (9 by 13 centimetres). Their advantage, apart from saving paper, was that these would arrive much faster than normal letters, but they also had to pass through censorship. Stella de St Paer still has a collection of the telegrams and the tiny airgraphs sent by her husband.

As local men went away, other soldiers arrived. John Mason, who was in the Regular Army, came back from India in 1939 with the Royal Artillery. He was posted to Ascot Racecourse to train new recruits. A few of the troops who came here already had relatives in the district. Joseph Wigmore's brother had emigrated in the 1930s but he returned to England with the Canadian Highlanders and was stationed at Chobham. He visited his brother in Cheapside arriving in a Bren-gun carrier to the great excitement of his nephews and nieces.

Some of the local young men were very eager to join the services. In spite of the fact that he had delivered some of the dreaded War Office messages during the school holidays and had been warned to leave quietly and not to wait for any replies, Gordon Butcher was one of those who longed to get involved. When he left school (in 1944) he found himself at the Royal Aircraft Establishment at Farnborough as a laboratory assistant. This was a reserved occupation but he volunteered for the Navy a day before his seventeenth birthday. The Engineering Department at Farnborough refused to release him for nine months when he finally managed to get into the Navy. He transferred to the Fleet Air Arm as an Air Mechanic, served for a year in the Far East and was demobbed at twenty.

There were exemptions from military service for all those who were in reserved occupations. These included a number of teachers, doctors, engineers, land workers and others regarded as essential to the economy. Those who refused conscription on conscientious grounds were called before tribunals and most were then drafted into non-combatant units and sent to work on the land and in forestry. There was a camp for conscientious objectors at Wentworth, Virginia Water, where they were employed building large underground offices, which may have been used if Whitehall had been abandoned.

Some of the older local men were sent to work on Directed Labour Schemes. Ian Cooper's carpenter father spent most of the war working at army camps leaving his motherless son with his grandmother. Many families were broken up in this way. But the majority of the men away from home were serving in the armed forces. Roy Grove was called up in September 1939 and joined the Royal Army Ordnance Corps. He did not go overseas but was posted all over England and Scotland and, like many others, he and his wife found that their first six years of married life consisted of a few fleeting visits. Mary's brothers were both in the RAF and her youngest brother was wounded. While her husband was away, Mary and her baby, like many others, returned home to live with her parents and unmarried sister.

Several local women served in the armed forces and a notable example was Maisie Hodder whose father Frederick kept the Post Office Stores in Sunningdale and was also the author of a history of the village. Maisie joined the Auxiliary Territorial Service (ATS) in 1942. Very soon after her enlistment she had a strange interview at Devonshire House Piccadilly where along with five others she was asked if she was sure that she wanted to do this work because if she started she must stay and could not be moved. With *"not the faintest idea of what it was, we all said Yes!"* Five weeks later they were all sent to Bletchley Park and allocated billets nearby in New Bradwell. In 1944 they were moved into the new military camp in Shenley Road closer to Bletchley Park.

Sunningdale Post Office

Maisie was in Captain Jackson's sub-section working as a decoder, initially on the *"double Playfair Code"* which was based on two squares of 25 letters of the alphabet, with no letter j. They worked twelve-hour shifts, four girls on each shift. The messages, intercepted from the German Military Police, were sorted at the intercept stations, sent to the code breakers at Bletchley, passed on with the appropriate code to the decoders, thence to the emenders and finally the decoded information was dispatched to the appropriate quarters.

None of decoders had any knowledge of German when they started but they soon understood most of the material before them. This usually concerned damage by Allied air raids and escaping Allied POWs and included the shootings after the Great Escape. Secrecy was the very essence of the job. Writing in the 1990s Maisie explained, *"we never spoke of work outside the office door and even now I find it hard to believe that we can talk about those days".*

EVACUATION

"Evacuate Forthwith"

One of the most overwhelming and significant aspects of wartime here was the immediate arrival of the evacuees. Indeed so many people moved out of London into this area that almost every household was directly affected.

The evacuation was not unexpected. All through the nineteen thirties as the country had gradually faced up to the prospect of a war with Germany, pessimistic and realistic opinions were being voiced. *"The bomber will always get through"* warned Stanley Baldwin as early as 1932. The civilian population would be targeted as never before. Huge casualties were expected from bombing raids and the raids would begin as soon as war was declared. Therefore national evacuation schemes and plans for air raid shelters were prepared well in advance. As well as the government schemes, many firms, private schools and other institutions made their own arrangements to move out of the big cities.

The Committee of Evacuation was established in May 1938 under the control of Sir John Anderson. The aim was to achieve the voluntary removal of 3.5 million people, mostly children, from all the big cities. It was a colossal project and was planned like a military exercise. There were 1,589 assembly points and 168 entraining points. Whole schools including teachers would be relocated and evacuation was also offered to mothers of under school-age children, pregnant women and the disabled.

East Berkshire was designated as a reception area for evacuees from London and 25,000 children were allocated to the whole area. WRDC began to organize for its share in the winter of 1938/1939. By May there were lists of people who had volunteered to take unaccompanied children and the Council had found places for 1,438 children, not far short of their allotted target of 1,600.

In order to encourage people to take in the evacuees the government paid a billeting allowance of ten shillings and sixpence a week for one evacuee and eight shillings and sixpence for the second or for younger children. There were many complaints that this was not enough to keep a growing child (the billeting allowance for a civil servant was twenty-one shillings). As a result of objections, the allowance was later raised to ten shillings and sixpence for all children up to fourteen years old. The parents of evacuees were means tested and were expected to make contributions of between nine and six shillings if they could. Since it tended to be the poorer families who opted for evacuation, more than one quarter made no contribution.

EVACUATION

By August 1939 the WRDC had devised a full evacuation scheme and had divided their area into five administrative zones: Sunningdale where the reception officer was H. E. Kite with ten billeting officers, Ascot and North Ascot with J. H. Nelson as the reception officer and 16 billeting officers, Sunninghill with H. Nicholson as the reception officer and 22 billeting officers, Old Windsor with A. Plumb as the reception officer and 18 billeting officers and Windsor Great Park as a separate area with J. Macmillan as the reception officer and with just 3 billeting officers. Into this last area, by far the smallest in the WRDC, came between eighty and a hundred evacuees from Stepney.

All the officials were volunteers and initially it was expected that they would be needed for only a short time. Eventually however the position of the billeting officer became a fulltime, paid job and offices were set up in Ascot and Sunninghill. Throughout the war anyone who had a spare room had to register with the billeting officer. The major tasks facing the officials in 1939 was to find sufficient accommodation for all the children due to arrive and to see that they were all safely delivered to their foster families. The WVS, Red Cross and WI were all brought in to help. An Evacuation Appeals Committee was also set up. Lucy Archer Shee of Ashurst Lodge, Sunninghill, joined this committee in September 1939. She worked tirelessly and sympathetically on behalf of the evacuees. Whenever evacuation in Ascot and Sunninghill is mentioned, Lucy Archer Shee is remembered with affection.

The great evacuation of London began on August 28th six days before the declaration of war. Although the schools were still on holiday, pupils and teachers had been recalled for a practice and then the order went out to *"Evacuate Forthwith"*. By the third of September, one and a half million had left London and the other cities. Within a month half of all the London school children were moved out and their schools transferred into the country.

Natalie Paknadel (then Rabin) remembers that her school, the Woolmore Street School in Poplar, was evacuated on Friday the first of September. She also recalled the *"slave market"* selection of evacuees. Arriving by train at Windsor Station, the children were brought to Sunninghill by bus and then *"touted round the streets of Sunninghill in a parade of cars which came to a standstill in Lower Village Road. A lady put her head through the window, pointed to me, then aged seven and a half and said, 'I'll have her and another one like her'. I immediately protested. I had with me two cousins, brother and sister, the boy just over a year younger than me, and his sister, two years younger still. I had promised my mother and my aunt that I'd look after them and keep us all together and I was determined to do just that. The lady, Mrs May Blay, was sufficiently impressed to take all three of us. After all we* **were** *cousins and could sleep in the same bed, which we did! I was billeted at 2, Addington Cottages, Lower Village Road opposite Sirl's the Coal Merchant and Removals Firm."* Albert Blay was a gardener and he had an allotment in the Bog where he grew *"amazing vegetables"* including beautifully blanched celery.

Evacuees were supposed to be kept in family groups but many were separated from their brothers and sisters. Charlie Piper from Poplar found himself in Windsor while his brother was in Sunninghill. When Charlie's family was bombed out of London both boys came to Sunninghill and after the war they all stayed on here and Charlie married a local girl.

Natalie was one of a small group of Jewish children, including her cousins, the Solomons, who came to Sunninghill and Ascot. In 1942 Woodcote on the Windsor Road in North Ascot became a Jewish Community hostel for children mostly from North London including many refugees. The 31 boys and 11 girls at Woodcote attended the Ascot Heath Schools. Their entry into school was delayed for several months until enough desks could be provided.

Natalie also remembers that *"After the war it* (Woodcote) *was used to house children, mostly boys, who had been rescued from Belsen. They were aiming to go to what was then Palestine. My parents were able to obtain the services of a young Czechoslovakian man to teach my brothers Hebrew in preparation for their bar mitzvahs. Later my parents joined the Staines synagogue where my brothers were bar mitzvahed".*

Percy Hathaway watched as a large number of evacuees were brought into Cromwell Road, South Ascot on the first of September and were allocated to the families there. These may well have included Natalie. The Hathaway family took in two evacuees Harry and Sammy Cole who came from the same school in Poplar. Later their mother and baby brother came too. Percy recalled that they were all unused to fresh vegetables and like many other evacuees they soon went back to London but returned later.

Some of the evacuees were brought into Sunninghill and Ascot by coach. Hazel Sharman remembers them coming in double-decker buses and George Laney went down to help carry the cases when the bus dropped the children off at Sunninghill crossroads. He felt very sorry for the little ones. Mavis Colman's mother went to collect one child but brought three of them home.

Four of those arriving on a double-decker bus on the first of September were the Sheppard children, George aged twelve and his sisters Joyce ten, Hilda eight and Margaret five. Joyce remembered that journey in great detail even after sixty-six years. They had left their home in Galsworthy House Stepney very early that morning. With other children from the Trafalgar Square School they were put on a very slow train to Windsor. The whole journey from school to Windsor took six hours. Each child carried a gas mask and a carrier bag given as they left school containing a bar of chocolate and a hard biscuit. Their clothes were in a small suitcase.

As they came out of Windsor Royal Station they were paraded in groups and put onto buses. The Sheppards lost contact with many of their school friends and found themselves on the bus to Sunninghill.

Upper Village Road Sunninghill 1941

When they arrived they were gathered in a group in Upper Village Road and waited to be collected. Joyce remembers that they were the last because the four of them were trying to stay together. This proved very difficult and finally Mrs Mitchell, a WVS member, took them all back on a temporary basis to her own home. Mr Mitchell was the cobbler in Upper Village Road. The Mitchells were always kind to the children and even after they moved away they still invited them back for tea. Eventually the children were split up. George and Margaret stayed with the Mitchells and Joyce and her sister Hilda went to stay with the Barfields, an elderly childless couple who lived in the same road.

The Barfields were very strict and Joyce and her sister were not at all happy there. Encouraged by a teacher to write home they did so and expressed their unhappiness. Their mother came to see them and the two girls were moved to another family. In the two and a half years before their mother came out to Sunningdale they had five homes. George was also homesick and with another little boy he set off to walk home to London but they were found and brought back. Their youngest brother William however had gone with his nursery school to Ipswich where he was very well cared for by an elderly couple who loved him dearly. He stayed with them for almost three years seeing his parents only once and he was very miserable when he was brought back to join the family in 1943.

Trafalgar Square Infant School, Stepney E.1.

Most of the children at this school was evacuated to the Windsor area. Hilda Sheppard and Joyce Smith came to Sunninghill.

In 1942 Mrs Sheppard suddenly joined the children in Sunninghill. After a night of heavy raids she had emerged from the Underground shelter with her older daughter Maud, her two-year-old Elizabeth and her new baby to find a sea of bombed buildings and dead bodies. Shocked and horrified they scrambled out and unable to see a way home she set off with her daughters to walk to Sunninghill carrying her baby. At night they sheltered in the Underground and during the day they were given food by passers-by. After three days they reached Richmond and from there they were helped to get a train to Sunningdale.

Mr Sheppard soon joined them for although their flat had been undamaged in the raid, one weekend when he came out to see his family in Sunninghill, thieves broke in and stole all their possessions. He was transferred from his job as a stoker at the Stepney Gas Works to the same job with much less pay at the Camberley Gas Works. He cycled there daily from Sunningdale. In the evenings he took on another job at the Hermitage Cinema where Joyce remembers he had to have a fine new uniform when King Zog (see later) paid a visit.

The Sheppards became the first family to be moved into Callaly, a fine old house in today's Whitmore Lane Sunningdale. It had been requisitioned by the WRDC. They were given the ground floor with a kitchen, two bedrooms and a bathroom. The girls had the second bedroom and the two boys slept upstairs until they went off to the army. Other families joined them at Callaly mostly using one room for each family. At the maximum there were five families, one of which had come down from Birmingham.

Most evacuated children however stayed with local families. The Butcher family in Course Road took in two evacuees, six-year-old Ronnie Brown and his friend Derek Schofield both from Poplar. They were brought to the house by Lucy Archer Shee, who was taking them from door to door. Gordon and his brother Alan begged his Aunt (who had looked after them since their mother died) to have the little boys to stay. Poor Ronny had eczema and his father was killed in the blitz. He was very nervous and very upset and didn't stay but Derek was there long enough for Gordon to teach him to read.

Enid Reeves (then Butler) remembers a group of tired little evacuees sitting down on the pavement opposite her home in Course Road. Her mother went out to collect a boy who would sleep in the bedroom vacated by her son, then in the navy. She returned with a boy and his sister, Lionel and Rosalind Crimholt. Enid had to make room for Rosalind in her room. The Crimholts were Jewish and at first their parents came down once a month to bring them kosher food but as the war went on they ate whatever was available. They stayed for some time and, when they left, the Butler family took in the wife of a Scottish soldier in the Royal Engineers who wanted to see her husband before he went overseas.

Not all of the children were carefully handed over. Edna Jakeman who lived in Cheapside Road had agreed to take in two evacuees. She came back home from work one day to find two little boys sitting on her doorstep with labels around their necks. They stayed with her for most of the war and were in touch with her for the rest of her life.

After the initial evacuation came the long period of the *"bore war"* or *"funny war"*, later to be known by the American name as the *"phoney war"*. In December 1939, the Vicar of St Michael's commented that many of the evacuated children had returned to London and that there had been no bombs on London at all. In fact during the first months of the war it was rather more dangerous in the countryside. By January 1940 almost sixty per cent of the evacuees had returned home. Margaret Finlay, wife of Hope Finlay the head gardener for Colonel Horlick of Titnest Park and Little Paddocks, had taken in two little girls from Hammersmith but they both went back home within a few months.

The bombing of London began in the summer of 1940 and the blitz was even worse in the early autumn. More than a thousand civilians were killed in the first half of September. As a result many of the evacuees returned often together with their mothers and grandparents who were bombed out. The Finlays received two more evacuees, this time two young boys from Poplar, George and Bobbie. They stayed for about eighteen months. Bobbie left to rejoin his parents in the west of England and George's parents, who had been bombed out of their London home, came to Sunninghill and he went to live with them.

Paul Snook's family was typical of the new evacuees coming into the area. His father was a monumental mason living in West Ham with his wife and six children. His eldest son was already serving in the Fleet Air Arm. One morning early in 1941 they came up out of the Underground shelter to find their whole street and home totally destroyed. The family were provided with a truck and told to drive west. When they reached Ascot his father stopped in the High Street, opposite today's Post Office, to buy cigarettes. As he got out of the truck an air raid warning siren went off. He hurried his pregnant wife and six children out and into the ditch at the side of the road. (There was then a ditch and a hedge all along the fields on the south side of the High Street.) Peering from the ditch he saw people ignoring the signal and walking along the pavement. He offered them a place in the ditch but was told *"Oh nothing ever happens in Ascot"*. *"This is the place for us"*, he said and the family went straight to the billeting officer. Faced with a family of eight the Council billeting office managed to find one room in a house in Nursery Lane North Ascot. Fortunately they were shortly moved into a three-bedroom apartment at Ashdown in Kennel Ride where the baby was born. The children went to Ascot Heath School and Paul started at the infants classes held in the Parish Hall, later moving into the main building of the boys' school in Fernbank Road. There all the London children were kept together in one class and even had their break times apart from the other children to prevent fighting. He remembers the local children lining the roadside and shouting at them as they left school. All the younger children were frightened.

Natalie Paknadel's parents also became victims of the blitz and her mother and two younger brothers joined her in Sunninghill. Her father, an electrician on the Underground, had to stay behind in lodgings. Natalie's family was billeted above the stables at Norton Grange in Morrison's Lane (now St Mary's Hill), an estate then occupied by Sir Edward Hoare. The drive up to the house was lined by magnificent mature rhododendrons but their living quarters, shared with three other families, were far from luxurious. They had only one room for the four of them and had to use a chemical toilet. As the blitz abated, the other families moved out or back to London and they were able to occupy all three rooms and were even allowed to use the WC that had until then been reserved for the gardener. There was no electricity or gas and the families used paraffin lamps and heaters. Her mother had to master the art of cooking on a paraffin stove. Their stark existence was eased by the kindness of Lucy Archer Shee who found an armchair for her mother. Like many families who had been bombed out, Natalie's family stayed on in Sunninghill after the war and eventually moved into a new council house on the Bouldish Farm Estate.

Another family member, Beila Rabin, came from Stepney in 1940. She was pregnant and was allotted a comfortable room at Frognal Lodge (the Marist Convent today) sharing the small house with three other families. Her baby, Naomi, remembers growing up on a farm rather than in a lodge on a large estate because most of the garden had been ploughed and was under cultivation.

Beila was just one of the many expectant mothers who had to move to have their babies in safety. The London Mothers' Convalescent Home already existed on the Chobham Road in Sunningdale and in the war years it was used more than ever. During the summer of 1943 and again in August 1944, when the V1s were falling, pregnant women were leaving London at a rate of more than 500 per week. It was not easy to find billets for all of them near London and some were sent as far away as Leicester and Derby. Those who came to Ascot and Sunninghill had to travel to Wokingham or Bagshot nursing homes to have their babies. Many of them stayed here until the end of the war.

Peggy & Arthur Clark

Two of the young evacuees who came to Ascot and eventually settled here are Peggy and Arthur Clark. Peggy Clark (then Peggy Headicar) was twelve years old when she came with her two younger brothers, Cecil and Richard, all evacuated with the boys' school, Christ Church School, Chelsea. It was a small school with three or four teachers. On the weekend that the war broke out they assembled at Tite Street and were sent by coach to Windsor. Her parents didn't know where they would be going but the children had postcards and were instructed to write home as soon as they arrived.

When Peggy and her brothers reached Windsor they were taken to Ascot Farm on Sunninghill Park estate. This was the home of Sir Philip Hill's bailiff, Mr Robert Finlay, *"a dour but kind Scot"* who had previously been a keeper of the Royal Horticultural Society Gardens at Wisley for twenty years. He and his elderly invalid wife and their daughter Jean, who was married to a Squadron Leader, took in seven evacuees. They were well treated and well fed but faced some culture clashes such as well-salted porridge for breakfast, which they decided was inedible, so they were given sweetened groats instead. The farm had the same facilities, electricity, WCs and baths as they had at home.

Shepherd White's Corner

Peggy remembers the excitement of having the run of the farm, climbing trees and making dens. She was a tomboy and loved the country life. Mr Finlay would take the boys with him on his shooting expeditions. Peggy and her brothers had a few very enjoyable months at Ascot Farm but with Mrs Finlay seriously ill they had to move on. This time they were billeted in two cottages (now vanished) near Shepherd White's Corner, the junction of the Winkfield and Windsor Roads. Peggy stayed with Archie and Doris Bowyer. Archie Bowyer worked at the gas works and they had two children of their own.

Her brothers were billeted next door but they proved to be too much trouble for the couple there. *"They were rascals, they made a den in the woods and when given a ferret by some American soldiers tried to bury it in a hole at the den but it escaped and ate some of Mr Bowyer's chickens before the cockerel managed to wake everyone up. What a catastrophe!"* The brothers also ate some chocolates left in their cottage and as a result they were transferred to the care of Wilf and Ethel Barrass in New Road. There they were well looked after but it was not a happy household so in the end the Bowyers took in the boys as well.

The Bowyers' cottage was not large but seven of them managed to squeeze in together. Once when the girls tried to change the beds around they ended up stuck fast on the staircase, unable to get up or down, until Archie came home to help. The Bowyers were a kind and very tolerant couple. Peggy remembers telling their children, Edwin and Doris, that if they dug deep enough they would reach Australia. So they dug in the garden all day long until they had such a huge hole that when Archie Bowyer came home from work and saw it, he thought it was a bomb crater. Mr Bowyer grew all their vegetables and kept chickens, successfully after the ferret had been well caged. Mrs Bowyer was a very good cook (later she was the cook at the Marist Convent) and the children had plenty of good food but Edwin ate everyone's butter ration because he couldn't eat margarine.

The cottage had no gas or electricity and all the cooking was done on the range. The house was very cold and once in trying to get close to the fire Peggy upset a pan of scalding porridge on her foot and was laid up for several weeks. There was a privy outside at the end of the garden and Mr Bowyer emptied the bucket. On Mondays, Mrs Bowyer did the washing in the copper and then they all used the water for baths. Peggy and her brothers had left a house in London with gaslights, a WC and a bathroom upstairs, for a primitive rural cottage but they had no complaints. It was *"a big adventure"*.

Many children like Peggy and the Sheppards found themselves living in cottages with far fewer facilities than they had had in London and local families such as the Lewis household in Sunninghill provided baths for some of the evacuees who had none in their billets. Hot public baths were also available in South Ascot. They had to be booked ahead through Mrs Gould at the South Ascot Billeting Office. The baths were open every day except Sunday, soap and towels were not provided and the charge was 4d for adults and 2d for children. There were of course also many children from London who found better conditions in the country than they had at home. The majority of the homes in Stepney had no baths but they all had modern sanitation..

Peggy's parents came out to visit at weekends whenever they could. The Government provided cheap day-return train tickets under the *"Visit an Evacuee"* scheme. Her father took them to church since the Bowyers did not attend. Peggy was confirmed at All Saints Church. Looking back Peggy doesn't remember feeling sad but she now feels very sorry for her mother who was devastated at losing her children. Peggy's main regrets were losing touch with her London friends and feeling very isolated. This problem was solved when she was given a bicycle on her thirteenth birthday.

As soon as she had her bicycle Peggy was able to help with a paper round at White Waltham, a round trip of about twenty miles. Her war effort consisted of unpicking old jerseys, knitting squares and collecting acorns for pigs. Peggy soon made friends with local girls, especially Vera Hathaway. On Saturday mornings they used to go to the Hermitage Cinema in Ascot to see *"Charlie Chan"* and other films. They also went to The Picture House in Sunninghill where Peggy remembered seeing *"The Four Feathers"*. Peggy stayed here until late in 1944 when she returned to London and became a typist.

Peggy's husband Arthur Clark had lived in a large basement flat at the Barons Court end of West Kensington. He was first evacuated when he was ten-years-old with the Star Road School, Fulham and taken by train to Peaselake in Surrey. He and his parents had no idea where he would be going but it was very exciting to live in the country. He was billeted in a lovely big house overlooking the centre of the village green with a large conservatory full of russet apples. He has good memories of eating apples and reading comics and although he was apart from his brother and sister he was quite happy. As the phoney war continued, he, like many others, returned home but when the 1940s blitz began Arthur was again evacuated.

This time a group of them came by bus to Sunninghill. Arthur and his brother Trevor went to stay with Mrs Willett in Station Road, Sunningdale. She had two sons and one was his age. After a short time they were moved to Beech Grove in Church Lane, Sunninghill, the home of Captain and Mrs Fullarton James and their daughter Isabel. *"It was magic!"* They had the freedom of the house and grounds. There was the Iron Bridge over the London Road, built in the nineteenth century to link the house with its woods beyond. Arthur could play there with his brother.

The Iron Bridge across the London Road

Beech Grove

Within the house they were looked after by Winnie, the senior maid. Arthur was allowed to use Captain Fullarton James' library and there he discovered *"the love of my life, reading"*. There were all the books a boy could wish for. Every Sunday, the Irish maid took them to Sunninghill Church and in the afternoon they were taken into Ascot to the Mascot Tea Rooms for tea and cakes. He also remembers going to Paynes, the sweet shop in Sunninghill, and buying Tizer, a new drink for him that *"seemed like nectar"*.

Alas this paradise did not last and they had to move again though he doesn't know why. They went to a cottage in The Rise at Sunningdale where the facilities were very primitive and they were not very welcome. He attended classes given by a Mr Henstridge who lived in Oriental Road and later went to school in *"a hut"* next to Sunninghill School. Eventually he and his brother were admitted to Sunninghill School. Arthur remembers that he had no trouble with the locals and experienced no animosity. The evacuees were just called *"townees"*. He made local friends and belonged to a gang who went to the cinema together. George Laney a local lad who became one of Arthur's friends, remembers differently. He recalled that there were plenty of fights between the locals and the outsiders which went on *"for about two years"*.

The Rise Sunningdale

Eventually Arthur's mother came down from London. His father was away in the army, and the family managed to get accommodation in Cheapside next door to the Post Office. They stayed there for about a year until they were allocated a council house in The Rise and it was there that most of his family was reunited. He remembered having a good time with the American airmen (see later) who let the boys go swimming in the lake at Sunninghill Park. His youngest sister became a GI bride and, when the war was over, she left for married life in America.

During the war Arthur also knitted squares, collected scrap metal, and gathered acorns to feed the pigs. On Saturdays he worked at Silwood nursery, weeding for a tanner a day. At fourteen he had a brief job as a trainee waiter at the Brook Club in Cheapside, but he didn't like the clientele and his employment ended when he tipped soup on *"a particularly nasty piece of work"*. He joined the Air Training Corps, the 1897 Squadron, at Dormy House in Sunningdale. There he had a great time. There were shooting practices, flights in airplanes from Blackbushe airfield, training trips to Lee-on-the-Solent and Portsmouth with the Navy and more training at RAF Halton in Buckinghamshire at an NCO camp. On his 16th birthday he volunteered for the Merchant Navy and joined the *"Vindicatrix"*. After a year he transferred to the RAF and went to the Middle East. By this time the war was over.

Both Arthur and his brother stayed on here after the war rather than return to London. His brother now lives in Bracknell and Arthur and Peggy settled in Ascot. The paths of Peggy and Arthur never crossed in wartime but they met when she returned to Ascot for weekends to see her friends and they both went to the local *"hops"* at the Cordes Hall in Sunninghill. They married, had a family and Peggy became a medical secretary at Heatherwood Hospital.

The Sheppard family also stayed here after the war moving into a council house in The Rise. Two of the Sheppard boys and one of the girls had joined the services and all but one married into local families, Joyce Sheppard marrying Victor Cook from Cheapside.

These stories are typical of the lives of many of the evacuees. Some must have been deeply upset at leaving their parents but children are very resilient as Peggy, Arthur, Natalie and Joyce's stories show. Most of them entered into the experience full of interest in their new way of life. Most were billeted on the poorer families. And most were moved several times before they had a stable home and some never achieved that until they were reunited with their parents.

EVACUATION

"How Ascot dealt with the children from London"

There were many shortages among the evacuees that had to be supplied either by their foster families or by charity. Some lacked suitable shoes and clothing for the countryside. Dressing a contingent of rapidly growing children was a continuing problem. George the twelve-year-old billeted with Margaret Finlay arrived with only the clothes he was wearing and these were very thin and shabby. Margaret managed to collect more clothes from within the large Finlay family and she persuaded Lucy Archer Shee to buy him an overcoat from WVS funds.

Of course many of the evacuated children's parents were willing and able to equip their own children but if they were bombed out they had to leave London with little more than the clothes they were wearing. Once more it was the WVS and the WI who stepped in, collecting and distributing clothes, boots and shoes as needed. During the last six months of 1940 more than one million pounds worth of clothing was sent over from Canada. It was all sorted and allocated by volunteers from these women's organisations. Mrs Fullarton James of Beech Grove and Mrs Gould in South Ascot ran clothes collections and shops to help the evacuees and their families in emergencies. Clubs were set up by the WI and the local churches to help the mothers cope with their many problems including the failure of the authorities to pay their allowances on time.

Although people could be fined for not disclosing that they had a spare room, the Council was hard pressed to find enough billets and there were constant appeals in the press. When there was not enough accommodation with local families, some groups of evacuees and evacuated families were settled in houses taken over by the WRDC (see Appendix II). Ascot Lodge in North Ascot and Callaly, where the Sheppards lived, were hostels for families. Other flats and houses such as Dale Lodge Cottages in Sunningdale were requisitioned for the homeless who continued to arrive from the London blitz. By the end of the war the council had acquired many more properties including the Food Control Committee premises in Queen's Road and the office manned by the WVS in the High Street at Sunninghill. Little Kames in Oriental Road became a home *"for difficult boys"* relocated from London. When they left at the end of the war the council congratulated the matron for keeping them all in order and out of public view.

It is difficult to know exactly how many evacuees were billeted here

29

and for how long. In November 1940, the Vicar of St Michael's noted the arrival of about *"250 more children"* and an ARP census of the same date claimed that the numbers of evacuees had doubled since September 1939. At Christmas in 1940, parties were given in Sunninghill for *"more"* than 550 evacuated children. According to figures collected by the WRDC in January 1940, there were 1,891 evacuees in the whole rural district but by spring 1940 there were just over a thousand evacuees left (for more detailed figures see Appendix III.) These numbers reflect the drift back to London. Following the heavier bombing in the city a thousand more children arrived at Windsor in June 1940.

The council's figures do not include the many who made private arrangements. Some local families took in relations or friends from London. Elsie Phillips' husband made an agreement with a friend at the pub. Two evacuees, a brother and sister, came to stay with her for two years until their mother came to join them and they all moved into local lodgings.

Certainly the councillors were alarmed by the numbers arriving. They doubted that the sanitary infrastructure could cope with all the new residents and sought assurances from the army that they would not billet any more troops in their area. In January 1940 the Council voted against using Torwood on the London Road in Ascot (already requisitioned by the War Department) as a home for nursery children because *"it was impossible to accept any more evacuees"*. Yet a few weeks later they agreed to the transfer of seventeen London children from Egham to Torwood, since there was nowhere else for them to go, but only on the condition that Egham Council took over responsibility for the house. Two months later the WRDC drew up plans to accept another 200 and to receive as many as 700 in transit if necessary. By July, as the second wave of evacuees flooded out of the city, the Council was considering how they might accommodate another 500 children and parents.

The stresses and strains of the evacuation system show not only in the widely varying statistics and the frequent movement of the evacuees themselves but also by friction in the administration. There was a major quarrel over whether members of the WVS could also serve as billeting officers. At the end of 1941 Mr J. H. Nelson, Mrs Gould and Miss Archer Shee were the unpaid billeting officers in this area. The Council was using the WVS office in South Ascot to keep the billeting records and to deal with any problems. This office was managed by Mrs Gould, who like Lucy Archer Shee was a WVS member.

In the spring and summer of 1942 the relationship between Mr Nelson, who was also the Chairman of the WRDC, and the other billeting officers deteriorated badly. In July Lucy Archer Shee, a councillor, resigned as a volunteer billeting officer because she had been appointed to a position at the WVS county headquarters. Mrs Gould who was unpaid was replaced by Mrs Cole who was to be paid a salary of three pounds six shillings a week. A new billeting office was set up in a shop in Sunninghill High Street rented by the WRDC at ten shillings a week. The area north of the London Road, previously run by Mr Nelson, was placed under another paid billeting officer called Mrs Watney.

The antagonism which had caused all these changes was aired at two angry Council Meetings in July and August. At the first, held in the absence of Mr Nelson, Miss Archer Shee put her side of the story. She protested at the treatment of Mrs Gould whom she claimed had not resigned but had been dismissed simply because Mr Nelson had unilaterally decided that billeting officers should not be members of the WVS She read out Nelson's letter to Mrs Gould: *"knowing you as I do it would be a stupid formality to thank you for all you have done as a Billeting Officer, but I think you know how I feel about it. Anyhow we shall be able to co-operate in other matters as in the past. Will you please return your billeting warrant to me at the end of the month?"*

The Council received several letters and a petition from 210 people in South Ascot against the closure of the office and the termination of Mrs Gould's position there. One of the letters came from the *"London evacuated teachers of South Ascot"* who were *"much perturbed and concerned at the termination of Mrs Gould's appointment as billeting officer"* because she had been *"a great success and had organised baths for adults and children, set up a clothing store, a village library and a soup kitchen which had been transformed into a dinner centre."* The soup kitchen may well have annoyed some of the councillors who had resolutely opposed all proposals to take responsibility for a communal kitchen. This had been proposed several times and the WVS had finally started providing hot meals for some of the evacuated families who had no facilities for cooking.

Miss Archer Shee challenged Mr Nelson's right to deal in such an arbitrary way in these matters but his authority was upheld by the majority in the Council. At the following Council Meeting he defended himself by stressing his authority as the chief billeting officer and asserting that everyone concerned with the evacuation, including *"Mrs Palmer, the County Organiser of the WVS, agreed that billeting and the WVS should be kept separate".* He added that he had had no co-operation from Miss Archer Shee since the Ascot district had been divided up. After lengthy discussions, Mr Nelson won his vote of confidence, Miss

Archer Shee was refused the right to reply and the matter was closed.

Considering the vast amount of work that Mrs Gould and Miss Archer Shee had undertaken on behalf of the evacuees and the admiration for Lucy Archer Shee that was expressed by everyone who remembers her, it does seem that these two had been treated pretty shabbily. Both Archer Shee and Nelson resigned from the Council in 1943. Nelson left the area altogether in March having sold off his home Woodcote to become the Jewish hostel. Lucy Archer Shee became a full time staff member of the WVS and continued to work for the evacuees through the WVS and the Red Cross. Mrs Gould also went on working for others and collected money for the evacuated families. In one year she raised a total of £1,600.

All the billeting officers were certainly under a great deal of pressure. At one time there were seventy complaints a day in the WRDC area and most of these came from landladies who wanted the removal of their evacuees. There were constant expense claims for the replacement of spoiled bedding, for broken chairs and torn wallpaper and even for a damaged bath. The complaints were so numerous that Lucy Archer Shee was asked to produce a report. The results appeared in January 1940 in *"The Windsor Slough and Eton Express"* under the headline *"How Ascot Dealt With the Children From London: Fifty per cent were Untrained and Verminous"*.

In fact the report specifically stated that following advice to the foster parents and, presumably as a result of sad and disturbed little children finally settling in, only three children had had to be sent to Bracknell hospital for treatment for bedwetting. But this had become a public issue and there was frequent publicity about it. In June 1940 an allowance of 3s and 6d a week was made available for householders whose evacuees suffered from this ailment. Margaret Finlay who had to cope with this problem with one of her evacuees had never heard of this allowance.

Miss Archer Shee also reported that the lice problem was due to the inadequate treatment provided by school nurses and she urged the use of paraffin which *"would cure 100 percent of the cases"*. There were only five cases of serious impetigo and three of scabies and she assured the committee that most of the evacuated children had excellent health. Indeed the report painted a much rosier picture than the headlines suggested. Not for the last time the journalists seem to have read a different report.

Hospitals, Homes and Schools

Private schools made their own evacuation arrangements. Eversley School, a small private school that had evacuated from near Lymington in Hampshire, came back from Cornwall in June 1943 and settled at Kings Beeches. But not all the traffic was in the same direction and Heatherdown School was one establishment that evacuated from Ascot to Shropshire.

Orphanages and boarding schools for the blind and the handicapped also came here. The Robert Spurrier Home for the Blind came to North Ascot and in the autumn of 1941 the Barclay School for Partially Sighted Girls arrived from Brighton to stay at Little Paddocks (now the Royal Berkshire Hotel). This school had been founded in 1893 and had 80 pupils. They stayed at Little Paddocks until 1962.

Kingswick South Front

Kingswick in Sunninghill became home to a London County Council School for disabled children and another LCC institution that moved to Ascot was the Stepney Geere School for Physically Defective Children. These thirty children, all with physical handicaps, moved into Daneswood, a large house in South Ascot, accompanied by their headmistress, an assistant teacher, a cook and three domestic servants. Eleven children who were brothers or sisters of these children but had no physical problems of their own were billeted nearby and went to

33

school at Daneswood. It was not a large enough house to accommodate a school of forty-one children and they were certainly neglected, a state of affairs that resulted in an indignant report from a Schools Inspector in February 1941.

The living conditions were poor and there was very little furniture. The children had to sleep downstairs so they could be rescued in case of a night raid and they took their lessons upstairs. The blackout made the rooms very dark, the electric light was too weak and the ventilation inadequate. Some of the children were short of clothes because their parents had lost everything in the blitz. The medical provision consisted of one LCC nurse for half an hour a day and the local doctor was reluctant to take on so many patients. The medical problems were finally solved by putting the school in contact with Heatherwood Hospital. The LCC admitted that the school had been forgotten and assured the Inspector that improvements would be made.

Heatherwood Hospital had begun as the result of the First World War and was greatly expanded in the second. It had opened in the 1920s as a United Service Fund Hospital for the children of ex-servicemen and women and was financed by the profits from running soldiers' canteens. Long-term care was provided for a hundred and thirty children suffering from orthopaedic tuberculosis. There was a full time school on the premises and the patients had their own Scout Troop. Older scouts from the Ascot troop would go along to help.

In 1934 the hospital had been handed over to the LCC. Though it continued to take in children whose parents had been in the armed services it also provided beds for other children with the same ailments. Extra wards were added and the numbers increased by a hundred. When the war began, the LCC was no longer able to send the older patients on to their hospital in Lowestoft so even more wards were added to Heatherwood.

The institution best remembered in Ascot was the Maurice Girls' Home of Ealing, one of the orphanages of the Church of England Children's Society, then known as the Waifs and Strays Society. These girls were expected to leave school at fourteen and go into domestic service but one of them managed to go on to teacher training college. This was Sheila Stewart whose book *"A Home from Home"* paints a vivid picture of their life here in Ascot.

The thirty girls arrived with their matron, sister and nurse on the Friday before the war began, coming here straight from their camping holiday at Great Holland in East Anglia. Their new home was at Englemere Wood, a large estate opposite All Saints Church. Sheila and the other girls were amazed at the prospect of expansive lawns, woods and a lake. They had the use of one large room to serve as a dormitory, a bathroom, a lavatory, a garden room and a dining room. An inspection by the Home Office reported that they were very cramped and needed more accommodation and after this they were given more rooms.

The owner, Mrs Peyton, was a cousin of Queen Elizabeth (later the Queen Mother) and she welcomed the girls on their first night. As a thank you to *"Madam"*, as they addressed her, the children cleared brambles and undergrowth in the woods and collected and cut up fallen timber. Mrs Peyton had two sons, John the eldest and, later, the M.P. for Yeovil, was taken prisoner at Dunkirk and the younger, Thomas Grenville Pitt Peyton, was killed in April 1942 during the naval attack on St Nazaire. His memorial service was held at All Saints Church.

The uniformed children became well known in Ascot as *"the Home Girls"*. Every weekday they walked in an orderly crocodile to Ascot Heath Girls' School. They also attended all the services and Sunday school at All Saints Church. Sheila remembered that each week the Rector would read out the names of the local men who had been posted as missing or killed.

Englemere Ascot in the 1930s

Back at Englemere Wood the girls trained for emergencies: trying on their gasmasks, learning their identity numbers off by heart and timing their drill for air raids and fires. Fortunately they had no first hand experience of the war. Sheila remembered only one bomb falling anywhere nearby. This was in the grounds of Heatherwood Hospital and caused no major damage. Some of the girls witnessed a dogfight between two planes and saw a body falling to earth while they were out brambling.

In their leisure time the girls were taken on long walks to the Copper Horse and to the partly emptied Virginia Water Lake in Windsor Great Park. The Cunliffe Owens invited them to Sunningdale Park to see films such as *"Mrs Miniver"* and *"The Snow Goose"* in their private cinema and each year they were taken to the pantomime at Windsor.

Much of their spare time was spent knitting for the troops. They did this between courses at meal times and while listening to Children's Hour on the wireless. Once a week the older girls attended a knitting party at Englemere. Engelmere had belonged to General Lord Roberts and is now the Headquarters of the Chartered Institute of Builders. During the war it was divided into three dwellings. The bottom floor was occupied by the Polish Count Roscinski, foreign minister to the Polish Government in exile; the middle by the Princesses Helena Victoria and Marie Louise, daughters of King Edward VII and Queen Alexandra, and the top floor by Sir Archibald and Lady Weigall. The Princesses had arrived here from London in June 1940 and they and the Weigalls were generous supporters of all the local charities. Vera Hathaway remembers going carol singing at Engelmere with her Red Cross Brigade and receiving *"a good donation"*.

The Princesses hosted the Maurice Home knitting parties and knitted along with the girls sometimes joined by Lady Grace Weigall who was in a wheelchair. The sea-boot stockings, scarves and balaclava helmets were piled high on the billiard table. While they knitted away they would be entertained by Lady Weigall's memories of when her husband, Lieutenant Colonel Sir Archibald, had been Governor General of South Australia and by the Princesses' memories of their grandmother Queen Victoria and their stories about their nephew the King. On one occasion some of the older girls were invited to tea to meet Queen Elizabeth and the Princesses Elizabeth and Margaret. At Christmas the Home Girls performed a nativity play for the Royal family at Royal Lodge.

The Home was supported by many local people as well as by the Princesses. Their patrons included friends of Mrs Peyton such as Mrs Tufnell, Lady Lever, Mrs Mark Ostrer, Dr Halley and Major Cyril Fyson the manager of Lloyds Bank in Ascot. Some of these people donated clothes *"with very high class labels"*, and some gave financial support. The Canadian Red Cross sent them *"Bundles for Britain"* which were fondly remembered for their very bright and exciting clothes. The local churches and clubs also raised money for the "Home Girls". In September 1942 St Michael's Church collected £900 for them. Every year the girls prepared the Christmas Appeal for the Children's Society. In response to all this goodwill the girls sent out thank you letters and made and sent hundreds of Christmas cards.

When the war ended Sheila was seventeen. The Maurice Home did not return to Ealing, where their property had been damaged, but took a lease on Sandridge, a large house opposite Englemere Wood next to All Saints' Church (now a Care Home). They called their new home Grenville House after Thomas Peyton who had been killed at sea. After her time at Teacher Training College Sheila met her future husband. It was from Grenville House that Sheila had a white wedding attended by all her many friends and patrons including the Princesses.

Giving me permission to use the material from her book Sheila Stewart wrote in November 2004:

"the older I get the more I appreciate all that the people of that area did for me and the other girls in the home. I am very fortunate that our evacuation to Ascot opened up a world of opportunity... ... that I would never have enjoyed if we'd been stuck at Ealing. I feel very guilty when I think of those who suffered because of the war whereas I benefited so much. It was the luckiest day of my life when we were evacuated to Ascot".

Refugees and Governments in Exile

Not only Londoners, orphans and patients found refuge here. As early as 1938, about twenty wealthy Czechs and Austrians came to stay at the Berystede Hotel.

The new arrivals had fled the Nazi annexation of Austria. Their coming saved the hotel which had been doing very badly during the depression and this was the start of a very busy period for the Berystede. Then owned by Trust Houses Limited it was a smart hotel with 45 bedrooms and several suites of rooms set in 32 acres of pinewoods. There were large gardens, two tennis courts and a putting green. During the war it became a refuge from London and a base for many foreign ladies known locally as *"the Old Girls".* These included the American singer Russell Ryan and Mildred Hotson, wife of the ex-governor of Bengal. The Grand Duchess Charlotte of Luxembourg and her husband Prince Felix, the brother of the last Austrian Empress, stayed in a suite with their six children. Later they went off to Canada and the

Montagues of Great Fosters Egham moved into the suite that they had vacated.

When the blitz began many wealthy people chose to stay outside London. Following the example of King George VI and Queen Elizabeth who often slept at Windsor, other heads or ex-heads of state also came here. King Zog of Albania, his Hungarian Queen Geraldine and their little son Alexander settled at Forest Ridge on the Bagshot Road. He had been invited to England by King George VI after the invasion of Albania and stayed at the Ritz in London before arriving in Ascot. From the Berystede he moved into his rented house. Described as *"a very small man with very large bodyguards"*, he brought his sisters who lived nearby at Lowood. Queen Geraldine was often seen in the local shops. She attended services at the Catholic Church of St Francis in South Ascot and visited Englemere to take tea with the Princesses. Aprilla Gilfrin who was a taxi driver at the Berystede remembers that in August 1941 King Zog's aide-de-camp, Bayram Neli, an Illyrian, told her that Roosevelt and Churchill were having a very important meeting in the middle of the Atlantic that very day.

The Berystede Hotel

After King Zog and his entourage moved out, the Peruvian ambassador lived at Forest Ridge and his son married at St Francis' Church. Staff from the Brazilian embassy occupied Ancaster Lodge in

Burleigh Lane and the Chilean ambassador lived in South Ascot.

Nine-year-old King Feisal of Iraq and his mother were at Grove Lodge in Winkfield Row with their entourage. The locals remember that there were always armed guards on the gate. King Haakon of Norway spent some time at Foliejohn Park. His son, Crown Prince Olav and his Foreign Minister, Trygvie Lie were based in London but they visited this area often and the Norwegian Shipping Mission had offices at Shrubs Hill House in Sunningdale. It was from there that they organized the Norwegian Merchant Fleet that was bringing vital supplies to Britain throughout the war. Many Norwegians also served in the British Navy and Fleet Air Arm and stayed at the Mission when they were on leave.

After the invasion of their country in May 1940, some of the government in exile from The Netherlands made use of the very fine house called Rosewood in Burleigh Road. Queen Wilhelmina herself stayed for a short time at the Berystede Hotel and Prince Bernhard regularly visited the Rokeby-Johnson family in their house in Cranbourne. Margery Haspels, who attended Ranelagh School, lived in the flat above the Durning Library and her father worked at the Dutch Embassy. Towards the end of the war ex-King Peter of Yugoslavia lived in Sunninghill with his mother Queen Marie and it was from there that he attended Clare College at Cambridge. Several of the large houses along the Windsor Road Ascot were occupied by Free French and Polish families. Many of these temporary residents stayed only for a year or so, coming and going according to their personal circumstances and according to the dangers of the war.

Most evacuees and refugees were here for only part of the war period but the population was increased by well over fifty percent. As the war went on even the official evacuees increasingly made their own arrangements. Many returned to London soon after the invasion of Europe but as late as March 1944 there were still 1,350 unaccompanied children and 132 mothers and families living in billets. In September 1944 the Ministry of Health issued a circular suspending all the facilities for evacuation and arrangements were put in place to return the remaining evacuees to their homes. Enid Reeves remembered her mother receiving a letter from King George VI thanking the family for billeting evacuees. Her mother was very proud of the letter and had it framed.

By the end of 1944 most children were reunited with their parents but many families who had been driven out of London by the blitz stayed on in lodgings. As military accommodation became empty some of these families moved into the old army huts. Eventually they were allocated council houses. A considerable number of those who had come to escape the blitz stayed on and settled here. With the war coming to an end, the WRDC was facing the difficult problem of providing enough housing for all those who intended to remain.

"Learning about nature's wonders"

Public Information leaflet No 3 assured London parents that their evacuated children would be *"well looked after"*, that any religious preferences would be fully accommodated and that their education would be continued as before. In many cases none of these promises could be kept. Mrs Potter of Cheapside entered her young evacuee at the local Church of England school. Later she was told that since the child was a Catholic she must transfer him to St Francis' School in South Ascot. This was too far away for such a young child so he remained at the Cheapside School.

Far from continuity in education many received a very disjointed schooling and this affected local children as well as evacuees. It had been intended that evacuated schools should be kept together in separate establishments but there was a great shortage of suitable buildings. For the first two or three terms of the war some children, both locals and evacuees, had to share existing school buildings. The school day started early and there was only one short break so that all the pupils could all get four and a half hours schooling.

Sunninghill School

Ian Cooper remembers watching two large cupboards being delivered to his classroom at Sunninghill. At the end of the morning all the desks were cleared and all the books were put away in one of the cupboards so that the evacuated school could get out their own books from the other cupboard and work away in the afternoon.

The Sheppard children attended half-day school at the Village Hall in School Road Sunninghill and their headmaster Mr Denmark presided over a collection of London children from several schools. In the afternoons they were allowed to sit and read in the grounds of Kingswick and Frognal, now the Marist Convent. Two of the London teachers were billeted at the Duke's Head in Upper Village Road and the children were also invited to sit in the garden there. All London children continued to follow the London syllabus and at thirteen, Joyce Sheppard passed the exam to enter a technical school. She was sent to the Shoreditch and Clapham College evacuated to High Wycombe and she was billeted there on a weekly basis. At the end of the war Joyce worked at the Norwegian Shipping Mission in Sunningdale.

In her first months here Peggy Clark also attended Ascot Heath School for half days. In the other half of the day their teachers gave them open-air lessons on the Racecourse. She remembers sitting on the Heath in her warm coat knitting squares. Mr Pickering, one of the LCC teachers, very kindly gave her lessons to help her to keep up the French which she had started in London but which was not taught in the Ascot school. Peggy then transferred to the Clapham Central Senior School for Boys located at Cranbourne School which agreed to take a few of the cleverer, older girl evacuees. She took her School Certificate and stayed on there until December 1944. At first she walked the couple of miles to school but her birthday bicycle was *"a godsend in more ways than one"*. Some of the classes were held in the British Legion Hall up the road, and Mr Beer the maths teacher who was a short man gave Peggy sixpence a week to borrow her bike.

Every church and institute hall in the area was brought into use as schoolrooms. The All Souls Church Hall in South Ascot was taken over by Christ Church School from Chelsea and this school took in other London evacuees living nearby. The Sunningdale Infants School moved into the Coronation Memorial Hall and their school was taken over by St Saviour's School, Poplar.

The Woolmore Infants School from Poplar was installed at the Comrades' Club in Sunninghill. Natalie Paknadel remembered they were *"all together in one long room. The platform at one end, with the piano on, served as the Headmistress' study. Her name was Miss Parkin"*. When the Woolmore infants reached seven they joined the Fulham School, installed in the Scouts' Hut. One of the Poplar School mistresses, Miss Saunders, moved with them. After the war Miss Saunders stayed on in Sunninghill and commuted back to Poplar every day for several years.

The London teachers certainly rose to the challenges facing them and responded to the new environment. Natalie Paknadel was taught to identify trees and flowers, toads, frogs and water boatmen. As she wrote in 2005: *"Much of that knowledge has stayed with me and indeed my enthusiasm for the countryside was born then and still remains. All things considered although I* **learned** *about the bad side of the war, the blitz, the dying, the holocaust and so on, my own lasting memory of the war was learning about nature's wonders"*. Natalie went on to Windsor County Girls School after passing the scholarship exam in 1943.

Since there were so many evacuees and since many mothers were working in munitions factories there was a great increase in the demand for school dinners. A meal cost 4d for the older and 3d for the younger pupils and was free for the poorest children. There were real difficulties in providing so many more meals not least being the lack of space in which to prepare and eat them. In 1941 Lucy Archer Shee and the WVS were called in to advise local schools. At Sunninghill the building where today's local library stands was taken over and used as a canteen.

At Cranbourne School there was a truly remarkable domestic science teacher, Miss Spencer. In addition to all her extra teaching duties and with no extra pay, she organised dinners for more than 250 children. Some of the meals had to sent up the road to the British Legion Hall. She trained the cook and assistants, prepared the menus, ordered the provisions, paid the bills and arranged the sittings and deliveries. Surely she deserved a medal.

From January 1940 milk was also provided, a third of a pint for half a penny and free for the very poor. There were often shortages and problems with deliveries. In 1942 some schools including St Francis' had to cope with the milk being supplied in bulk due to the shortage of milk bottles. Teachers were told to use a measure to serve the milk into mugs the children had brought from home. All the children in Berkshire were also issued with free Horlicks tablets.

There was a constant worry that children would not reccive enough to eat and fears of an increase in diseases and epidemics due to the *"doubling of the child population of the district"*. The frequency of school medical inspections was increased and swift action was taken if any dangerous ailments were identified. When there was an incident of scarlet fever at Ascot Heath School all the girls from the Maurice Home were kept away from school. There were also regular testing and immunisation clinics at the schools to protect against diptheria, a scourge of the 1930s.

As well as having to find enough seats and enough space to teach and feed the children, the teachers were also expected to support the many fund raising campaigns. They sold National Savings Stamps and took children to patriotic celebrations for Empire Day and War Day parades. In Warships Week Ascot Heath schoolchildren went to see *"Forever England"* at the Hermitage Cinema and during Victory Campaign Week they watched *"In Which We Serve"*.

Schools had also to survive the call up and subsequent absence of teachers. At Sunninghill the headmaster Mr Harrington, who had already served in the First World War, was called up as part of the Royal Artillery Reserve. He returned within two years because of his age and the desperate need for teachers. He was one of the very few male teachers left in the area. There was also an absence of caretakers and cleaners. Sometimes senior girls took over the cleaning, being paid at the rate of five shillings a week.

When the evacuation period came to an end and the schools returned to London, not all the evacuees were able to go home and each school had a small number of children whose homes had been destroyed and whose parents were now in the area. Alfred Page remembered that twelve of them were left behind at the All Souls' Church Hall. They were given the choice of going to Sunninghill or to St Francis'. They chose the latter because they were afraid of the Sunninghill children who had often fought with them.

In spite of all the problems good teachers were still able to give special help when it was needed. Sheila Stewart had passed the scholarship exam when she was in Ealing. She had not been allowed to go to the grammar school because all the girls were expected to go into service when they were fourteen years old. Miss Cory of Ascot Heath School intervened on her behalf and with the support of local patrons and extra Latin lessons from the Rector, she was sent first to a boarding school where she was very unhappy and only lasted a term and then to Ranelagh Grammar School at Bracknell. Ranelagh had 180 pupils in 1939 and 308 by 1946, so much were the local school numbers increased. There she was made welcome, soon had some good friends and did very well. Eventually she went on to Teacher Training College all the while getting financial support from many well-wishers in Ascot.

Ascot Heath School

The impact on local schools is clearly shown in the records of Ascot Heath Girls School. This school and the Ascot Heath Boys School occupied the buildings used today as a private nursery school and a library in Fernbank Road. The two schools took pupils from the age of five to fourteen. Miss Cory, the headmistress of the girls' school, is remembered as a very competent teacher but she had a particularly difficult war. In 1939 she already had problems with the local management board and especially with the Rector, the Reverend Walton who had tried to get her removed and who continued to visit the school and criticize her on a daily basis.

The school was put *"on a wartime basis"* in September 1939 and the numbers on the register rose from 110 in July to 182 in September due to evacuees from London and the girls from the Maurice Home. Sheila Stewart remembered the school was so overcrowded they were sitting four to a desk. In July 1940 it was even more crowded. By then, there were 229 girls in the school due to 59 new arrivals from the Rockmount Girls and Infants School of Croydon and another 21 arrived by October of the same year. This was the peak of the school roll and the number registered dropped back to 187 by the summer of 1942.

Ascot Heath Boys and Girls Schools

There had to be a considerable rearrangement of classes to accommodate the increased numbers. Three infants classes were set up in the Parish Hall, fifteen minutes walk away, and two classes were taught in the same room. This resulted in strong protests from local parents and some of those whose children had been moved to the Parish Hall removed their children from the school. Some classes were taught off the premises for part of the day. Miss Tilly, the infants' teacher, taught knitting, gardening and music in her own home next to the school. Older girls attended Ranelagh Grammar School for cookery and housewifery lessons. Later in the war they went to Cranbourne School for these subjects. Nature walks and swimming lessons at Bracknell also took the children out of the crowded premises. They travelled to Bracknell on the local buses, 2d there and 2d back.

January 1940 was a very harsh winter, the school was cold, the outdoor lavatories froze and in the end the school had to be closed for several days. In June 1941 Miss Cory was obliged to write a letter apologising for seeming to be *"rebellious and impertinent"*. This may have been because she complained that the stirrup pumps for fire fighting were unsatisfactory and she also pointed out that desks had still not arrived for the evacuees who had already been in the school for a term.

As well as actually teaching the children the staff had to train the children in the use of gas masks. *"The children must be broken of the habit of fiddling with their gas masks"*, was one of many notes made by the Rector in the school log. Older girls were shown how to use the stirrup pumps and there were regular air raid drills, sometimes supervised by the ARP. Peggy Clark remembered that they had air raid drill every Friday when they all had to wear their gas masks and since there were no shelters the children crouched in cupboards and under desks whenever there was an air raid siren.

None of the local schools had air raid shelters. It may seem strange that there was no effort to protect the children especially as the numbers were so swollen by the influx of evacuees. The advice of the Home Office put the responsibility for all safety on the shoulders of the Local Education Authority and the school governors. Since this was designated as a rural area where bombs would not be targeted, there was no *"justification for any considerable expenditure on shelter provision"*.

All the school buildings in Sunninghill, Sunningdale and Ascot had high windows. These were covered with wire netting and taped to reduce the dangers of flying glass but this also made the classrooms much darker. There were also plenty of suggestions as to other measures that schools might take for themselves. A government leaflet of 1939 has a two-page appendix on the construction of slit trenches, arched shelters and sandbag walling. Not surprisingly none of the local schools dug up their playgrounds to make trenches. By 1941 the officials of the Department of Education seemed to have changed their minds about trenches too and more sensibly advised that all schools should be equipped with a wireless. Teachers were also instructed to warn the children about the small anti-personnel mines. These were only five or nine inches in size (thirteen and twenty-three centimetres) and would be very attractive to curious children.

Generally schools were expected to improvise during air raids. Sunninghill had a cellar under one of the classrooms. This was sometimes used as a shelter, the children sharing it with the coal. At the start of the war whenever there was a warning all the infants at the Sunningdale School were taken to shelter in a corridor at the back of the building. It was roofed with corrugated iron and had no lights and some were afraid to go inside. Sheila Stewart recalled Miss Cory at the Ascot Heath School debating with the Rector whether the pupils would be safer under their desks in the middle of the room or beside the walls. The Ascot Heath girls were ultimately instructed to lie down or sit up *"one foot from the walls wearing their gas masks".* The Reverend Walton suggested that all the pupils should keep iron rations in their gas mask boxes in case of a disaster and that the teachers should check these every day.

By the end of 1940 there had been so many air raid alarms and so little damage that it was decided to keep the children working during air raids. The nearest the Ascot Heath School came to actual damage was in November 1940 when the school was closed for a day because there was a time bomb in the vicinity. The only war damage to the school came in March 1944 when two tanks skidded on to the playground during manoeuvres and broke the main manhole cover.

St Francis' School

The only local school to be hit by a stray German bomb was the Catholic School of St Francis at the Friary in South Ascot. Other bombs fell nearby in the woods at the same time. Fortunately the raid occurred at five thirty in the early morning when there was nobody there, but the school buildings were almost entirely demolished and the pet tortoise was killed.

St Francis' School was already very much on a war footing and had

had a very busy year. In September 1939 a new headmistress had arrived taking over from Mother Bonaventure who had been there for many years. Immediately Miss Creagham had to cope with the arrival of two evacuated schools, Wendell Park, Hammersmith, a Mixed Junior School, bringing 38 children and Christ Church School, Chelsea, a boys' school with infants, juniors and seniors, bringing 39 pupils. Together with their own 65 pupils this small school was impossibly full. They adopted the shift system. After one term during which the St Francis' pupils attended until lunchtime and the evacuees took over for the afternoon, Wendell Park School was given the large hut which had served as a gym and the Chelsea school moved out into the All Souls' Parish Hall in South Ascot. By 1940 when many of the evacuees had returned to London, the Wendell Park School had joined them there. There were very good relations between the host and the evacuated schools. In December 1944 the St Francis' children were guests when the Wendell Park School performed scenes from Peter Pan and in April 1945 they all enjoyed a Handel concert.

St Francis' school-log records the disruption caused by air raids. On the first of October 1940 the headmistress wrote: *"Many children unable to sleep in last night's air-raid. Some have stayed at home"* and a year later she added that there had been *"two day time alerts one in the morning, the other just before 4 p.m.".* Again in February and June 1944 heavy air raids were keeping the children up at night and causing them to miss school the next day. Generally school attendance figures were low during the war.

When the bomb destroyed the school in November 1940, the pupils joined the evacuated schools in the All Souls' Parish Hall returning to a regime of half days. After a few months of this they were relocated into the *"Manual Workshop and Women's Institute Hall"* an old building behind Sunninghill School. The furniture and books that had been salvaged from the ruined building were taken over and the school reopened in early December.

St Francis' shared the playground with Sunninghill School using it at different times to avoid overcrowding and fights. Sunninghill School was also very full at this time. There were many problems for the staff and pupils in the Institute, as it was called, an antiquated heating system, a shortage of blackboards and reading books and no equipment at all for the infants. But the teachers were soon busy with Christmas parties, visits to the cinema, fund raising for the war effort and collecting salvage. In December 1943 the younger children were invited to a memorable party at the USAAF base at Sunninghill Park.

Long after the war ended St Francis' School remained at Sunninghill in the Institute building described in a school report as *"a wretched hovel"*. There were some efforts to improve their education such as swimming lessons at Little Paddocks but it was a constant battle for the head and the staff coping with all the problems of this very old and badly maintained building. When they finally left it was demolished and is now the site of a car park.

It was not until 1953 that the St Francis' School was able to move back to its old site in Coronation road and then only into temporary huts. These included two old army huts from Sunninghill Park that had already been used as temporary housing. It was 1962 before they were promised a new school building and this was not completed until 1967.

Although St Francis' was the only school to be bombed all the local school were very hard stretched by the conditions of the war. Any pleas by the head teachers for more desks and materials to cope with the extra pupils were dealt with extremely slowly. Evacuation affected not only the evacuees themselves but also the children in the local schools who had to share their facilities and teachers with them.

Although some children soon became friends with the evacuees others were disturbed when their parents had to take in strange children and they themselves had to move out of their bedrooms to make room for the newcomers. This was often resented and so were the treats which often went to the evacuees and not to the local children. It was natural to organise Christmas parties for the children who were away from their parents or whose families had lost everything in the London Blitz. But many local children had parents away in the armed services or working far from home and they did not share in the parties and treats. Sometimes this caused friction among the children themselves, seen for instance in the fights remembered by George Laney and Alfred Page and in the shouting at the evacuees remembered by Paul Snook. At first the evacuees tended to regard the local children as rural yokels and they in turn were seen as rough *"townees"*. Nevertheless as the Clarks and Snooks remember, generally everyone got along together. After all they had many shared problems and as everyone knew *"There was a War on"*.

THE HOME FRONT

"What To Do In An Emergency"

As the evacuees and refugees arrived and the service men left, the locals adjusted their lives. The outbreak of war had arrived after a very long period of uncertainty. Many people had become so used to foreign crises that they thought the Polish invasion would also be solved without fighting. But there were many others who had realised that, in spite of the *"Peace in our Time"* agreement of 1938, war with Germany could not be avoided. Parliament was recalled on the twenty-second of August and swiftly passed the Emergency Powers Act, the basis of all the wartime regulations that would affect everyone's lives.

The Old Court House

By the time war was declared, most adults were braced for the inevitable. The first sign of the coming dangers came immediately after the Prime Minister's broadcast when the air raid warning signals were tested. The Ascot siren was on top of the Old Court House, then the main Ascot Police station. A regular Magistrates Court sat there. (Another court met during the four days of Race Week at the Metropolitan Police Barracks where today's Police Station is sited.) As well as the Old Court House siren, air raid warnings came from the steam hooter at Sunninghill Gas Works, several short blasts for a warning and one longer blast for the *"All Clear"*. The Sunningdale siren was near the railway station.

Early in 1940 a sixty-four-page booklet entitled *"What to do in an Emergency"* dropped through all the letterboxes. This was a graphic account called *"The Jones family sees it through"*. Readers were shown how to make protective garden trenches and surface shelters, instructed in the duties of the Air Raid Warden Service and given information about rescue services, the clearing of debris, ambulance services, the auxiliary fire service, first aid posts and the decontamination squad. One thing people would not be short of during the war was advice from the Government. The 1940s saw a flood of regulations and advice. Some people recall that their parents were worried by the alarming possibilities described in the leaflets but many said firmly that they always put Government leaflets in the bin.

The WRDC had to ensure that all the new regulations were enforced within their authority. The Council had already assembled stores of blankets and piles of sandbags. Important facilities including police stations, telephone exchanges, electric transformer stations and sewage works were protected with sandbags and barricade blocks. Immobilisation schemes for petrol stations were prepared ready to be executed in case of invasion.

The Government decided that hump-backed Anderson shelters should be delivered free to all households with an annual income of less than £250. By September 1939 nearly two million shelters had been distributed. It cost the WRDC almost £6,000 to supply their area. Those who did not qualify for one made their own arrangements. The most rudimentary were trenches topped with corrugated iron and earth. More sophisticated were blast walls. Percy Hathaway's family in South Ascot, the Butcher family in Course Road and Elsie Phillip's family in Cheapside all had blast walls. These were six feet high and made of hollow cement blocks filled with earth and piled on top of each other. The walls were sited so as to protect the main windows.

Richard End dug a shelter for his family in the garden but after a year it was full of water as were many others in the low-lying districts. Joseph Wigmore built a very substantial shelter in the garden at Providence Cottage in Cheapside. He and his son slept in it for much of the war but his wife, their daughters and youngest son stayed in the house sleeping downstairs in the dining room. Later in the war some people had Morrison shelters, free to those on incomes less than £350 per annum and costing £7 to others. These were heavy iron tables with a solid iron base and four strong iron legs. They filled a small room and many women remember tearing their clothes on the roughly finished edges.

The majority around here had no shelters of any kind. Many people simply slept under their beds or under the stairs. John End recalled as a very small child being put to sleep under his cot. Roma Browning remembered sitting on a hundredweight sack of ground rice, sheltering in the larder with her Aunt and Grandma who shivered so much that she was terrified too! As in the schools, some windows were taped and netted to prevent the glass shattering. Fire buckets full of sand or water were kept near the doors. The best protected residents were the employees and ex-employees of the Ascot Racecourse Authority who were provided with a large shelter behind The Stag Inn. Enid Reeves remembers that whenever there was an air raid warning the family ran there from her home in Course Road.

Of all the war measures, the blackout had perhaps the greatest impact on every single inhabitant. Some of the hamlets had no streetlights but in the centres of Sunninghill, Ascot and Sunningdale the few lamps that there were went off. Car lights had to be dimmed and during air raids torches and bicycle lights had to be turned off. Louis Russell, then aged ten years, remembers watching a neighbour blacking out his car headlights on the day after war was declared.

The importance of hiding all domestic lights was explained in Public Information Leaflet Number Two in July 1939. This provided advice on making and fitting blinds and a recipe for making black dye for curtains by using a large amount of lamp black and concentrated size. New black sateen was available at two shillings a yard and could be used as a lining for existing curtains. Those who could not afford the new material dyed their existing curtains or sheets or used old blankets and made do with these.

Some like the Russell family made light wooden frames covered with roofing felt and attached these to their windows. Hazel Sharman's father also attached the blackout material to a frame and fastened the frame to the window with catches. It was lifted off during the day. Blackout had to cover all the windows unless like the End family in Sunningdale you had shutters. They moved down to the ground floor for the duration of the war where there were heavy wooden shutters. Even then they were once warned that a light was showing. It came from a grating high up in the kitchen. This was a serious matter and there were fines of up to £50, about £2,000 today, for anyone who offended three times. Many people were charged at the Ascot court for *"permitting a light"*. In 1941 Colonel Tufnell was fined £10. Another regular offence was for having no rear light on a bicycle.

Driving along unlit roads with seriously reduced car lights was difficult and dangerous. There was a hundred percent increase in road accidents in 1939. From January 1940 motorists had to reduce their speed to 20 mph in all built-up areas but it was only the reduction of traffic due to petrol rationing that prevented many more deaths. Various organisations such as the WVS ran courses for those who had to continue driving, such as doctors. There were constant letters in the press urging people to wear white capes at night. Women's organisations also promoted the whitening of all steps, kerbs, path-edges and drives to help to prevent accidents. The All Saints Church Magazine of March 1940 suggested the use of white Cardinal Polish that would not wash off in the rain.

To ease the problem of the darkness the Government retained summer time during the winter of 1939-1940 and this was doubled the following year. Clocks were put two hours forward from May to September, later in the war from March to September. This continued until 1945. There was however one real advantage from the blackout. The beauty of the night sky was revealed in all its glory and many people became very interested in astronomy.

In September 1939, following the National Registration Act, free identity cards were issued and about the same time gasmasks were distributed. These were either delivered to each home or had to be collected from the local village halls and schools where there were demonstrations on how to use them. Special baby gas masks were provided. These were large boxes into which the baby would be inserted. Richard and Florence End had one of these for John. They kept it beside his cot but fortunately never used it. Small children had Mickey Mouse gasmasks in pink or blue boxes.

John End in a Gas Mask

Two million of these had been distributed by January 1940 and there were tears when, at age seven, they had to be handed over for larger ones in plain brown boxes. Children had practices at school and there were competitions to see how long it was possible to read while wearing one. It was difficult to see through the masks because they misted up inside. Clever people smeared the inside with soap to prevent or at least to delay the misting up process. A few people however admitted that they never even tried them on.

"Unnecessary railings"

As well as introducing blackout, gasmasks and shelters the onset of the war brought many changes to the village landscape. One of the most dramatic alterations was the removal of railings that were a major characteristic of this area. These ranged from the modest rails and gates of cottages and terraces to the great gates and rails of parks and estates. Early in 1940 it was made compulsory to collect all *"unnecessary"* iron railings *"for the war effort"*.

Railings at Sunningdale Park

Grand and beautiful gates and railings were taken from Sir Hugh Cunliffe Owen's Sunningdale Park and from Hill Hampton house on Charters Road belonging to Lord and Lady St Oswalds of Nostell Priory. Smaller properties such as the terrace houses in Course Road, Sunningdale High Street and Cheapside Road lost their railings too. This destruction caused great resentment and still angers those who were there. Mary Grove recalls her annoyance at losing the small railings and gate of their house in Sunningdale. Mary Wood and several others remember that a crowd gathered at the Sunninghill crossroads. Some were very upset and others were shouting angrily when they cut away the large gates and high railings around Kingswick, destroying what had been a very impressive entry to the village. At the time there was a feeling of injustice because the Victorian Golden Gates at the entry to the Racecourse in Cheapside Road were left intact.

While the iron from the railings was being collected in July 1940, there was another appeal for aluminium to be made into Spitfires and Hurricanes. Many families handed in their saucepans but there was little logic in this collection. The shops had plenty of new aluminium pans for those who could afford to buy them. Like the removal of railings it was a misguided campaign promoted heavily by Lord Beaverbrook and Stella Lady Reading of the WVS. Most of the railings and pans were simply left in dumps since the metal was largely unusable for armaments.

In 1941 the WRDC resolved to inform the Ministry of Supply that they considered there was no point in collecting more scrap metal until the existing dumps were cleared. They also pressed the ministry for an elucidation of the phrase *"unnecessary railings"*. By February 1942 the Reverend Thursfield was writing that *"there are said to be thousands of tons of waste metal lying about all over England"*. Many of the railings were eventually replaced by chestnut paling fencing and John End recalled seeing German POWs working on this in old Sunningdale towards the end of the war.

Another very annoying change came at the end of August 1939 when the Government ordered that all place names *"visible from the air"* should be removed. This included all the railway station signs and added to the problems of train travel in dimly lit carriages. The elimination of names and signs went further and led to the removal of all the signposts and even some of the old milestones on the A30 and the London Road *"as if invading armies would have no maps or instructions on how to find London"*. By May 1940 there was a regulation that there should be *"no name signs on posts or shop fronts nor any indication of the distances to any place"*. Like many of the regulations this was carried through in a haphazard manner and by 1943 some of the signs reappeared. On the London Road through Ascot and Sunninghill at least one milestone giving the distance to Hyde Park was left in place and is still there.

The landscape was also transformed by the drainage of the larger lakes and ponds to prevent their use as navigational aids by enemy aircraft. There were lakes on many estates but the largest of all was Virginia Water. After it had been drained, there remained two shallow ponds full of pike and tench, to the delight of the local poachers. Both Virginia Water Lake and Wick Pond were drained in 1940 but the latter was refilled shortly afterwards. Weeds and new copses of trees sprang up in the empty mud of Virginia Water. When the lake was refilled in 1945 the public were allowed to bathe in it. It had to be drained again in 1947 to repair damage to the Cascade and after that public bathing was forbidden. Not all local lakes were drained. Sunninghill Park Lake remained full and was well used as a swimming pool by the local boys and by the American soldiers later in the war.

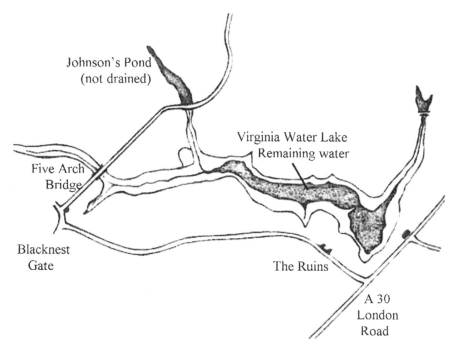

Virginia Water Lake drained during the War

Most of these changes arose out of a determination by the Government to be seen to be doing something and were also part of the panicky response to the threat of invasion after the defeat in Europe. There was also a powerful fear of spies, *"a fifth column"* of traitors, who were plotting to aid the Germans. Locally however there seems to have been very little alarm. Everyone knew the July 1940 slogan *"Careless Talk Costs Lives"* and they were careful not to speak out in public though most were unaware that there had been a £50 fine for passing on rumours likely to cause alarm and despondency. *"There were no spies here"* and *"we were ready for them"* were the phrases used when remembering this dangerous period.

"Most people were in uniform at some time or other"

Ascot and Area Special Police Force

Back, from left: unknown, Miller haberdasher Sunninghill, O'Donnel gardener, Ted Readings gasworker, Walter Bowyer Slough factory worker, Frank Sirl coal merchant.
Middle: Woolatt grocer Ascot, unknown, Pennicott butcher South Ascot, unknown, unknown, Frank Durman tailor at Weatherill's, PC Wells, Tom Goddard gardener, unknown, unknown, unknown, Oswald Mold, unknown.
Front: unknown, unknown, Chapman ironmonger, Bert Challis, Inspector Whitfield, Alf Goodchild upholsterer, Inspector Day, Billy Grimes mechanic, unknown, Poulton, unknown, Richard End photographer.

There was a vast array of men on the home front serving in the uniforms of the Special Police, the Auxiliary Fire Service, the Home Guard or the Air Raid Patrol. The Specials wore police uniforms, the Home Guard wore khaki and the Air Raid Patrol (ARP) and Fire Service wore navy blue.

Many more Special Police were recruited in 1940 and there were half a dozen of them in Sunningdale alone. These Constables co-operated with the regular police, the ARP and the Home Guard and went on patrol around the village. They were on a roster to be called out whenever they were needed. Richard End was a Special Constable in Sunningdale. Since many of them had no phone at home, they had to wait in the Home Guard dugout near the telephone box when on duty.

The ARP had been established by act of Parliament as early as 1937 and recruitment began in 1938 when Hitler marched his army into Austria. The ARP's duties were to enforce the blackout and coordinate the activities of all the other services during air raids. One of their more unusual duties was to paint selected pillars and posts with a special paint that would change colour if gas were present in the air. Many men had been recruited by October 1939. Although women served in the ARP in some towns and also often acted as drivers for the ambulances there seem to have been no women in the local branches.

Recruitment for the Auxiliary Fire Service started at the same time as the ARP was being formed. Before the war the Ascot Fire brigade like many others had been a voluntary body locally known as May's Brigade because it was run by Harry May, his three sons and his son-in-law with a few other volunteers. In 1939 it was taken over by the National Fire Service but continued to operate with the same personnel and from the same Fire Station at the eastern end of Ascot High Street.

All these organizations had to cooperate very closely. The Ascot ARP post was in the present day Chancellors Estate Agents (then Budgens) and the manager of Budgens was the head warden. They used the May's Garage in Winkfield Road and the Ascot Fire Station in the High Street as bases for their patrols. Gordon Butcher was a Boy Scout messenger for the ARP. He was paid half a crown for the use of his bike and later when he had proved reliable he was also recruited as a police messenger. Not all men served in the local auxiliary forces. Mavis Colman's father was one of the many who went from here up to London to serve in the ARP and he worked long hours as a stretcher-bearer during the blitz.

The Home Guard developed out of the Local Defence Volunteer (LDV) Force jokingly known as *"Look! Duck! Vanish!"* or *"Last Desperate Venture"*. This had been created in response to Tom Wintringham's campaign to create a Citizen Army ready to fight as a guerrilla army in case of invasion. Alarmed at this independent venture the Government took control and, on the fourteenth of May 1940, Anthony Eden appealed for volunteers to join the LDV Force. Within twenty-four hours of the broadcast, boys and old men formed long queues outside police stations waiting to sign up. More than a quarter of a million volunteered. The Government was totally unprepared for such a response and there was a scarcity of all equipment especially weapons and uniforms. Appeals were made to the public asking them to donate their shotguns and old World War uniforms were dug out of chests and cupboards.

On the thirteenth of June 1940 a leaflet entitled *"If Hitler Comes"* was sent to every household. Many people certainly remember being very frightened by its alarming tone. It was this leaflet that led to the acceleration of the removal of place names, the building of barricades and the rapid expansion of local LDV units. By August 1940, Sunninghill LDV Force had been formed with Sir Archibald Weigall as Commander and a formal inspection of the brigade was held at Sunningdale Park. The LDVs were soon in action manning the defences and obeying Government Directives.

Sunningdale Home Guard Dugout and Machine Gun Post with Special PC Oswald Mold

Pillboxes and defensive positions were established either with concrete or with mounds of sand bags filled by local boys on Crown Hill, loaded on to Albert Biddiscombe's lorry and delivered to all the designated sites. There was a chain of defence posts around the area: two in Cheapside, two in Old Sunningdale, several in Ascot, including one on Ascot Heath, and four in Sunninghill.

There were two machine-gun posts, one beside the old iron bridge on the London Road near the Sunninghill crossroads and the other at the corner of the Royal Ascot Hotel in Ascot (today the Heatherwood Hospital roundabout). These positions would be manned every night, during exercises, during air raids and of course in case of invasion. Road barriers consisting of tree trunks on large iron wheels were prepared and placed beside roads. Trenches were dug across side roads. Jars and tins of rusty nails and tacks were kept handy ready to be thrown in front of invading vehicles. If there was an invasion all the bells would be rung and at once the LDVs would rush into action. The ARP and the LDV Force were also instructed to check that all cars stored in garages had been properly demobilized. In July the LDV Force was renamed the Home Guard. Throughout that summer more uniforms and arms were supplied, many of the latter coming from the USA.

Women were not allowed to join the Home Guard though some had been members of the original LDVs and some typists and telephone operators were taken on as auxiliaries. The activities of the *"Lady Homeguarders"* of Sunningdale are recorded anonymously in the book, *"Berkshire Within Living Memory"* compiled by the members of the Berkshire Women's Institutes in 1996. *"We were not given uniforms nor even an armband but a large ornate broach to wear. We were, I suppose, a bit like Tolkein's dwarves, grudgingly acknowledged but seldom seen and rarely remembered. There were two of us in the Sunningdale contingent - me a rookie telephonist just completed six weeks training at Slough exchange, and my companion, a trainee schoolteacher. They needed us to man the phones. We were in the charge of Sgt Jack Barratt, a much liked and respected GPO engineer. We were taught the Morse code and had a tapper each for practice and some Sunday afternoons we did rifle practice with the men at Sunningdale Park".* The author of this extract also took part in a night training skirmish with a unit of Canadian soldiers from the camp on Chobham Common. The thunder-flashes of the Canadians proved to be much more powerful than those of the local Home Guard and indeed caused a real injury but it was not too serious. At dawn they all crept *"silently over the back gardens to the rear of the Nag's Head, where the landlord was waiting with large tankards of time honoured refreshment".*

There were three Home Guard units around here. Mary Grove's father, Mr Boswell, was in the Sunningdale Unit. As well as skirmishing with the Canadians this unit would practise in Blacknest Road (now Whitmore Lane) where they erected concrete bollards across the road forcing everyone to walk through the neighbouring garden of Ravenswood House.

Bill Sarney told John End about his memories of the Sunninghill Home Guard. Their headquarters was in a two-storied wood and corrugated iron hut at the Dearman's Builders Yard in Queen's Road.

There was a small armoury protected by breeze-blocks downstairs and a club upstairs with a bar that sold beer and filled bread rolls. They shared these premises with the Sunninghill ARP and their surviving register reveals a vigorous sale of drinks. The Sunninghill sentry points were in the High Street next to the railway bridge near today's pharmacy, beside the railway bridge in Upper Village Road near the Dog and Partridge Inn and at the south-east corner of the Berystede Hotel. This last was the most unpopular because it was the furthest from headquarters and from the pubs.

Roy Morton also recalled this Home Guard platoon in some detail and according to his record (deposited with John End): *"Mr Ferris the Manager of Berystede Hotel who had been a Captain in World War One was the CO. He was so thin that he was known to the lads as the 'pull through'* (pull-throughs were used for cleaning rifles)*".* Gordon Butcher pointed out that Mr Ferris was a short fat man and that it was Major Needham a commander of one of the platoons who had the right physique for a pull through. Roy continued: *"the second in command was also an ex-World War One Captain who lived at Early Dene, Bagshot Road. Another officer was Frank Oldham the engineer at the Sunninghill Water Works and another lieutenant was George Day. The sergeant Armourer was John Hunt a watchmaker from Upper Village Road and he spent more time at Queen's Road than in his own shop. The Platoon Sergeant was a man from Holmes Dairy in Winkfield Row. Once a week when he was on duty he would bring a piece of fresh haddock for everyone. Among the men were Mr Miller, a draper and a perfect match for Mr Godfrey in 'Dad's Army', an ex-London PC who was a proper spiv, Mr Sexton of Oriental Road and Mr Bowyer of Sunninghill."* A risky asset was *"Charlie Cooper who caused a near accident when he did not clear his rifle properly and nearly shot a mate in the head. When we were on guard duty a regular visitor was PC Argent from Oriental Rd who always arrived when tea was brewing".*

Roy also remembered the weekend exercises lasting from Saturday noon to Sunday noon. The Sunninghill unit would defend checkpoints at the Sunninghill and Berystede crossroads from the Ascot Home Guard Company. Some of these exercises were run by Captain Fullarton James of Beech Grove. On these occasions the HQ and the Red Cross Station would be in the billiard room at Beech Grove. The WI and the Red Cross supervised by Isabel Fullerton James supplied and cooked *"resplendent breakfasts".* For transport on these exercises they used two Sirl lorries driven by Pedlar Hopkins and Charlie Sillett who were Sirl's drivers. They also made use of private cars loaned for the duration of the war.

Ascot Home Guard Machine Gun Crew at Little Paddocks

The regular evening training was at Frognal on light nights and in winter they stayed in the Queen's Road having weapon training and drill downstairs. Upstairs there were training talks on grenades and explosives given by Jack Stevens. Extra training was given at the Bisley Ranges on Sundays with a *"haversack lunch"* provided by the regular army and a mug of something hot at the end. *"These days would end with a shoot off for a sweepstake and if there were Ascot, Sunningdale, Sunninghill and Chobham taking part it was a good sweep to win. I won it twice"* wrote Roy.

Relatively unscathed

During the summer of 1940 the Battle of Britain raged across southeast England. Although this area was relatively unscathed compared to nearby London there were more than twenty-five raids between August and December 1940 and over a hundred high explosive and many more incendiary bombs fell around here. 1,310 bombs fell across the whole of Berkshire in this period. Most of these were the result of *"tip and run"* raids when bombs were jettisoned by enemy planes escaping from Allied fighters. There were several dogfights in the skies over here.

Aprilla Gilfrin remembers *"the Polish squadron shooting up the Germans in broad daylight"*. This was probably the particularly frightening air raid that hit Sunningdale on September 9th 1940 at about five in the afternoon. A group of Heinkel bombers was intercepted by a Polish Spitfire squadron. It was thought that the bombers were aiming for the aircraft factories at Weybridge. There was no air raid warning until the fight was well under way. Louis Russell remembers being in his garden at Windlesham and being told to lie down flat on the ground by his anxious father. The bombers scattered and dropped their loads of about eighty bombs across Sunningdale, several exploding on the golf course shattering all the glass in the clubhouse windows.

George Laney and his brother were out on their paper round and were eagerly watching the chase between Spitfires and German bombers. But when they saw the machine gun bullets flying past their heads, they were suddenly frightened and as the bombs were jettisoned a neighbour pulled them into his homemade trench shelter. They fled home when the earth began to fall in on their heads.

Station Parade, Sunningdale in 1936

Mary Grove remembers the same afternoon. She was wheeling her baby home from her parents' house in Shrubs Hill Lane to the High Street in Sunningdale. As she went on her way planes began to come down low over the houses and some of them were dropping bombs. Terrified she fled into the home of friends in Bedford Lane and with her baby in her arms she joined them under the kitchen table.

Three oil bombs and seven high explosives fell on South Ascot and Sunningdale that day. A deliveryman from Cantrell and Cochrane, the soft drinks factory at Staines, was killed near the Sunningdale station. Crown Court bottle tops were scattered over a wide area. A second man who had just left the train and was waiting for a bus to Windlesham vanished into thin air. His body was found two days later on the roof of the Bank in Station Parade.

These daylight raids were particularly alarming. Several women remember being terrified and becoming very nervous. Children had to be kept close to home for fear of raids. Florence End recalled sitting in the family shelter with her small son quivering at the drone of the planes and thumps of the bombs and begging *"no more bangs Mummy"*. Between the summer of 1940 and spring of 1941, wave after wave of bombers continued to come in heading for London often via Reading or Windsor and the intercepted planes would drop their load as they fled. There were more fatalities in Fernbank Road North Ascot and in the Great Park.

In August several bombs hit Cowarth Park and left a large crater in Blacknest Road near the corner of Kiln Lane in Sunningdale blowing glass out of the nearby windows. In November, bombs dropped on the North Gate Lodge of Windsor Great Park and Joseph Pearce who was at home enjoying his leave from the army was killed. Before the end of the year another cluster of bombs had fallen in Ascot leaving a series of craters in gardens along Winkfield Road. Miss Chetwynd, a stalwart parish worker, filled in her crater with a new flowerbed planted with flowers to form a large V for Victory. Landmines were dropped too and one of these exploded near Dormy House in Sunningdale destroying a house in Ridgemount Road.

Another intrepid lady was Didi Andraea of Priory House Sunningdale. She was a very keen gardener and especially proud of her fine rockery. A bomb fell and lodged itself among the rocks, the fins sticking up above the ground. A bomb disposal squad arrived and told her she would have to leave the house because when they blew up the bomb there would be a large explosion. Didi was indignant. If Hitler had failed to blow up her house and garden the British Army would not be allowed to succeed. She refused to let them to start work and after a fierce argument sat down on top of the bomb until they agreed to allow her to make a phone call to a friend in the War Office. Didi lost no time in contacting her friend who told the bomb disposal squad to leave and sent out a disabling team. They safely defused the bomb saving her rockery. Parts of the disabled bomb rusted away behind the garden shed until the house was sold off thirty years later.

In September 1941 a bomb fell close to St Michael's Church Sunninghill leaving a thirty foot crater just outside the west end. It damaged the tower, blew out parts of the stained glass windows and demolished some of the vaulted graves in the churchyard. The locals were intrigued to see that one of the graves disturbed was that of a German lady who had lived in the parish many years previously.

Bomb crater at St Michael's Church

Percy Henry Crutchley, whose family had owned Sunninghill Park since the middle of the eighteenth century, died shortly after the bombing of the church. The day before his death at the age of eighty-five, he attended a meeting to discuss the damage. His son Commander Victor Crutchley offered to pay for the repairs to the tower in memory of his father. By January 1942 the church had raised most of the £700 required for all the repairs. By June the structure had been restored but the windows had to wait until after the war when some of the costs would be met by the government.

1940 and 1941 were such bad years for raids that some local children went off to stay with relatives further from London. Some went as far as the United States or Canada but the danger of crossing U-boat infested seas deterred many families. Roma Browning went for her holidays with an aunt in the Lake District and remained there for more than a year because it was so much safer.

At first none of these raids were reported in the press for national security reasons. *"We had to be like Dad and keep mum"* was the slogan. As time went by however there were more and more references to the difficult conditions under which everyone was living. In the Parish Magazine of November 1940, the Reverend Thursfield gave thanks for *"many miraculous escapes"* following bombs in Winkfield Road near the Racecourse and at Kingswick where there was an evacuated school for crippled children. Later in 1941 the local press reported the death of a woman *"whose home, at the Shepherd White's Corner, Ascot, had been damaged by a bomb in September 1940"*. There were also appeals for furniture for air raid victims and reports of fires.

Bomb damage at St Michael's Church photographed by the young Trevor Lewis. Note gasmask boxes.

A few enemy planes came down in the district including a Messerschmitt ME 109 which fell in the Great Park. In April 1941 a Heinkel HE 111 crashed near The Crispin Inn in Woodside. George Laney and his brother tried in vain to steal a piece with a swastika on it and were chased across the fields by the police. One or two bits of that plane did end up in local homes. Two of the crew were killed and were buried in Brookwood Cemetery and two were injured and taken prisoner.

Some of our planes came down too. Early in the war a Spitfire crashed near Sunningdale station. In the winter of 1943 there were two more, one was a Stirling Bomber that fell between Ascot railway station and Heatherwood hospital. An American Flying Fortress also crashed in a field along Winkfield Lane. Fortunately the crews survived most of these accidents. Vernon Cox remembered sitting on the doorstep in Sunningdale watching four of our bombers coming back. They were heavily damaged with broken undercarriages and one was on fire. As they flew over, slowly and unevenly, he wondered however they would get home and however they were going to land.

The only air defence system near here was the anti-aircraft battery on the Review Ground in Windsor Great Park, at the east side of Queen Anne's Gate. It was equipped with six guns and was permanently manned. There were living quarters and a sergeants' mess on the site as well as a small landing strip marked out for a light aircraft. Beside this was a mobile barrage balloon unit and the whole area was heavily fenced with barbed wire. The searchlight was on the other side of the road nearer to Flemish Farm. Twelve-foot poles were driven into the ground to prevent enemy planes landing on the Cavalry Exercise Ground nearby. Three defence pillboxes were also set up around the Park. There was a second search light unit near Woodside staffed by members of the ATS who lived in adjacent huts when they were on duty.

There were also a set of diversionary lights on Chobham Common south of Sunningdale, intended to draw the bombers away from their London targets. Since planes attacking London often came in over Sunninghill, Sunningdale and Ascot the local population became very used to air raid warnings on most nights. But they knew they were luckier than the Londoners for if they looked east they could see the red lights from the terrible fires in the city. From his home in Trinity Crescent, Adrian Turner remembers seeing the Sunningdale church spire silhouetted against the blazing sky. The old nursery rhyme had a chilling contemporary ring.

In the last year of the war, from June 1944 onwards, it was the V1 and V2 rockets that were especially worrying. The V1s, known as doodlebugs, were frightening but at least people could hear them coming. One hit the Bells of Ouseley in Old Windsor and two people were killed. Another landed in June 1944 not far from the Royal Lodge in the Great Park. A month later the elderly Countess Roberts, the daughter of General Roberts, had a close shave in her home at The Camp (now Whiteladies) in South Ascot. At a few minutes before seven in the morning a V1 demolished most of her roof and only the ceiling over her bed was left intact.

The V2 rockets made a silent approach and the first ones in September 1944 were announced as *"gas main explosions"* in the press. Very soon everyone knew that a nasty new menace had arrived. More than one thousand V2s fell in the following six months, the bulk of them on London. As well as the loss of life they made even more people homeless and many of them came here looking for accommodation of any sort. One V2 exploded in the air and the tail section came down in a field off Bagshot Road, beyond the Berystede Hotel, providing another attraction for local boys who tried to climb inside. Another V2 came down about 70 yards from the Obelisk in the Park.

By December 1944, however, there was the feeling that the worst was over, although V2s would arrive as late as March 1945. Lights were allowed to go on in the main streets for a short period at Christmas and the two electric lamps in Church Lane Sunninghill were switched on for Sunday evenings services at a cost of one shilling per Sunday. In April 1945 most of the Blackout Regulations finally came to an end and there was a great relief that the fear of air raids was over at last.

"Doing Our Bit"

While the men at home served in the Specials, the Fire Services, the Home Guard and the ARP, many of the women joined up in what was called *"the fourth line of defence"*. These were the Women's Voluntary Service, the Red Cross and the Women's Institute. All these organisations were kept busy throughout the war helping with the evacuated families, raising war funds, collecting used clothing and doing anything else that was needed. During the early years of the war they arranged lectures at the Cordes Hall and at WI meetings on air raid precautions, anti-gas measures, first aid and home nursing. They were expected to help with special target weeks and were particularly busy in 1943 with the Book Week. Hundreds and thousands of books were collected, sorted and sent to the armed forces, to hospitals, to blitzed libraries and for paper salvage.

The WVS was a nationwide organization, founded in 1938 by Stella, Marchioness of Reading who was the widow of a Viceroy of India. (It became the WRVS in 1966.) Like the WI it was distinguished by its lack of ranks and the willingness of everyone to roll up their sleeves and do any job that was needed. Their motto *"we never say no"* and their green tweed uniforms were very well known around here. After Dunkirk and the return of the Expeditionary Force they helped to run the canteens for the troops. By August 1941 there were almost a million members (eventually 1.3 million) and most of them were busy helping with the evacuation and assisting families who had been bombed out.

Throughout the war they also worked hard sewing miles and miles of camouflage netting, hard and dirty work.

The WVS shared an office with the Red Cross in Sunninghill High Street. The Red Cross was responsible for issuing orange juice, blackcurrant extract and cod liver oil to young children and pregnant mothers and caring for the health of evacuated families. They also distributed clothes and food, ran war saving clubs and collected money for the Penny a Week Fund, which was spent on comforts for the service men and women. Teams of workers were sent to wherever they were needed. This included helping the old and the sick and cooking meals for children's homes. Many young girls like Enid Reeves and Vera Hathaway became Red Cross cadets. They went regularly to the Barclay School at Little Paddocks to bathe the children and put them to bed so that the staff could have a night off.

Mavis Bagshaw of Sunninghill worked for the Red Cross both before and after her marriage to Frederick who was in the army and away all through the war. She had no children of her own but she *"nursed and fed a great many of other people's children"*. All through the war years, Mavis rose very early to cook breakfasts for the children at Little Paddocks, Englemere Wood or at other homes for evacuated schools and she *"never knew when she would get home at night"*. Mavis remembered working with Lucy Archer Shee, one of the pillars of the local WVS and *"such a hard worker and such a lovely lady"*.

Many women and girls sewed and darned socks for soldiers billeted in the area. The old tongue twister of the First World War was back in vogue, *"sister Susie sewing shirts for soldiers"*. A notice went up in the window of one South Ascot cottage saying *"Socks Darned"* only to be replaced a week later by another saying *"CLEAN Socks Darned"*. Enid Reeves (then Butler) met a Royal Pioneer soldier while she was playing outside her home in Course Road. He asked her if she knew anyone who could darn socks and she volunteered her mother who was not very pleased to be presented with large bags of holey socks. But the work became worthwhile when the soldier paid for the darning with packets of tea, sugar and bacon, *"enough for half the road"*.

Women and girls played a very important role in the production and preservation of food. They maintained gardens and allotments while their men were away, collected brambles and mushrooms, made nettle soup and gathered rose hips to be manufactured into rosehip syrup, a valuable source of vitamin C. Members of the WI made jam in large quantities which was sold for various war charities. If the jam did not set, it could be sold to schools.

Recommended Knitting for the Troops

Knitting became the main national occupation for women and girls and for some of the older men. Wool was rationed to two ounces of wool for one coupon but it was possible to get twenty-one ounces coupon-free wool if the knitting was for the forces. This scheme began in June 1941. Some of the wool seemed to be going astray so after a year the coupon free wool was made available only to knitting parties. Members of a recognised working party had the right to buy and wear the badge of the Voluntary Workers for the Forces. The WVS and the WI supplied the wool and told the knitters what to make. They knitted to order and were careful not to waste wool. The Official Guide *"Knitting for the Army"* issued *"with the authority of the Director of Voluntary Organisations"* warned that *"some fighting man will go short of a much needed warm garment every time a woman knits in a careless, haphazard manner"*. The same guide carried letters from General The Viscount Gort who had led the Expeditionary Force in France, from General Sir Alan Brook and from Lieut-General C. J. E. Auchinleck assuring the knitters that their warm gifts were very useful indeed and much appreciated.

In Sunninghill, the Girl Guides gathered at their leader Miss Ellis' house to knit mittens and socks and in so doing they won their own knitting badges as well. Some women joined knitting circles in Cheapside, Ascot and Sunninghill but many especially those with small babies still knitted at home. It is hard to imagine the amount knitted. Did anyone even try to quantify it? By the end of 1940 the Fairfield Knitting Party had produced 1,935 knitted articles and a further 10,000 bandages, dressings etc. Cheapside Working Party produced 3,214 garments in six months up to June 1941. Miles of khaki and navy blue wool were transformed into jerseys, pullovers, gloves, scarves, balaclava helmets and socks on their flying needles. As well as knitting for the troops they made hundreds of garments for bombed out families and for the evacuees, not to mention supplying their own families as well.

Of course there was plenty of time to knit at night. People didn't go out very much. There was little public transport and because of the blackout and air raids it was not very safe. In cities and towns, criminals took advantage of the darkness to snatch purses. In rural areas there were more road accidents due to the blackout. Nationally 600 were killed every month. The barred headlights on vehicles reduced visibility and the roads were in a bad condition after the harsh winter of 1939 to 1940. It had been so icy that *"you couldn't even walk on hands and knees"* said Aprilla Gilfrin. *"The one brightness around here at night"* she added, *"was when the Windsor Park search lights lit up the Park"*.

The war changed life dramatically for many women and girls. On a national scale, seventy-five per cent of paid jobs now had to be done by women and even women with young families were encouraged to go out to work. The Ministry of Health Circular No. 2435 encouraged Councils to establish nurseries for the children of mothers working in factories or in domestic work in hostels and institutions. In this area there were two residential nurseries and a day nursery. Early in the war the Westbourne residential nursery for babies and children up to five years old was moved from London into Udimore in Burleigh Road and this became known as the Udimore Nursery. Girls from Ascot Heath School knitted toys for the babies and toddlers to play with. The other residential nursery was at South Grange in the Bagshot Road Sunninghill. The day nursery was at Burleigh Wood in Burleigh Road. Many mothers preferred to leave their children with their own mothers or sisters if they could. The provision of nurseries was an additional expense for the WRDC and after the war both residential nurseries were rapidly closed. The day nursery became a nursery school and this moved into the South Grange premises.

As men left for the armed forces there were many gaps at work and in the community that had to be filled. Edward Duckett the choirmaster and organist at St Michael's Church was called up and Isabel Fullarton James, who was a Royal College Organist, took over his work. There was a dramatic increase in opportunities for women. Nationally the numbers in domestic service dropped by seventy-five percent. In these parishes where domestic service had been almost the only paid employment for women the drop was more like ninety percent.

Mary Wood had been a parlour maid and when war began she was called up. She went to the tribunal at Reading accompanied by her mother who was very ill with asthma. As the only child of a sick mother and with a father hard at work on the railways she was allocated to a home job and became a post-woman, delivering the mail in Ascot, North Ascot and Cheapside.

Each day she reached Sunninghill Post Office for 6.30 a.m. After sorting the mail she set off on her bicycle round which lasted about three and a half hours.

Mary Wood in her Post Office uniform

Like so many of her contemporaries she was of course in uniform, a very smart navy with a red trim. When the Americans first arrived at Sunninghill Park, Mary was chosen to deliver their locked mailbag and had a pass to take it through the gates and up to the main house. Mary was warned by the Postmaster never to talk about her work and she took this very seriously: *"after a training in service I was used to see all, hear all, say nothing"*. Later the Americans had very much more post and used to collect it themselves.

Several business firms moved here from London. One of these was the General Film Distributors, which occupied Swinley Hurst from 1941 to 1945, and offered secretarial jobs for local girls who, before the war, would have gone into service. Vera Hathaway had a job here and after the war she would travel up to London on a daily basis, something that would have been unthinkable for a girl in the 1930s. An extra bonus for these employees was the very welcome food parcels sent to all the English staff by their American counterparts.

Other offices and firms arriving in the district and employing women were the British Controlled Oilfields Offices at Spring Grove Sunningdale and the British Electrical and Allied Manufacturers at the Red House in Ascot. The Offices of the Rhodesian Railways were at Englemere Hill and later the Victoria Falls and Transvaal Power Company moved there.

Women and girls also worked in the munitions factories. The few local factories that existed before the war had generally employed men. Now they were converted to war work and had to take on women workers as well. Irene Jones and her sister cycled from Sunninghill to Virginia Water to work at Gavin Frank's factory, where they made screamers for bombs. It was heavy work, cutting, painting and baking these metal skirts. Irene recalled that the smell was horrible especially when she became pregnant. They worked twelve hour shifts, a fortnight of days followed by a fortnight of nights.

Long hours were the norm at every level of employment. In 1944, Mr Toy the Sewerage Engineer for WRDC commented that he had had no holiday for five years. He was seventy-three at the time. Irene Jones' husband worked at Long Cross repairing tanks and often had to work a double shift. Many local men and women worked long shifts at the munitions factory in the *"U.S. Concessionaires Pontiac Factory"* in Fernbank Road Ascot. In South Ascot the tailoring firm of Weatherill's kept fifty or sixty people busy making jodhpurs and uniforms for the army. Every Christmas they gave a big staff party which was a highlight of the year. They employed young lads from the Gordon Boys Home in West End, Chobham.

There were many small munitions works scattered around here, including one at the Sunningdale Motors in the London Road Sunningdale. There the lathes worked nonstop turning out components probably for the Wellington bombers being assembled in Windsor Great Park. Jacobs and Young, another firm which converted into manufacturing aeroplane parts, had moved here away from the London bombing. This factory was near the old Court House on the London Road in Ascot. Enid Reeves' father who had been a painter with the Ascot Authority worked there and so did John Mason's wife. They made rattan and cane frames for the wings of Mosquitoes. This firm was also well known for its popular concert party which performed at many fund raising events.

Even firms that did not make uniforms or armaments were involved with the war effort. The large sawmill in Shrubs Hill Lane was kept busy by the constant demand for wood. Most of their production went directly to the armed services. The other sawmill in Sunningdale, near the southeast corner of the London Road and Chobham Road, made pontoon rafts for D-Day.

Castleman's Builder's Yard in 1981

All the old employers had to keep going with fewer men. The Ascot and District Gas and Electricity Company maintained supplies with a skeleton staff. Local builders such as Castleman's (yard in Queen's Road and shop in The Terrace at Sunninghill) lost many men to the services and were left with older workers and apprentices. They, like Dearman's (which also had its yard in Queen's Road), had to send teams of workers up to London to work twelve and fourteen-hour days dealing with bomb damage. The workmen's train left Ascot at seven each morning and was always packed.

Due to the shortage of manpower there were long hours at the railways too. Mr Why, a railway worker, often had to do double shifts because there were so many troop and supply trains going through. Many people in all walks of life took on extra jobs. The Vicar of St Michael's Sunninghill became the chaplain to all the Forces in the area who had no regular military chaplain.

In Windsor Great Park, the level area, now the Smith's Lawn polo field, had been used in the 1930s as an occasional airstrip. The Prince of Wales (later Edward VIII) had found it convenient. During the war with the deliberate dispersal of aircraft and munitions factories it became a well-concealed Vickers-Armstrong factory. There were two heavily camouflaged hangers and grass runways. Sixty-four Wellington Mark VIs were assembled on the site and flown out by the Air Transport Auxiliary Service. The house named The Flying Barn is a souvenir of those times and stands close to the end of the main runway.

From 1941 these runways were also used by the Tiger Moths of the Elementary Training Camp that operated from Fairoaks Airfield at Chobham and from Charlie Watson's airstrip on Winkfield Plain, a satellite to Fairoaks. Later the 27th Transport Group of the USAAF occupied the north end of Smiths Lawn near the Cumberland Gate with their Stinson Sentinels and Cessna Bobcats. All this area was closed to the public but not to local boys who seem to have had plenty of opportunities to spot the aircraft from underneath the bushes.

Those who were boys in the war years remember these days as full of excitement. Boys and girls of thirteen and over were allowed off school to help with the harvest. They relished the interruptions to school though they do remember learning patriotic verse and national anthems. The pupils at Sunninghill School were taught the French National Anthem. George Laney could still remember it perfectly in 2005 and it was the only French he ever learnt. Most lads took a keen interest in everything to do with the war, marking up maps on their bedroom walls and collecting shrapnel and cap badges, the latter were worn with pride mounted on their belts. They collected anti-radar paper with its interesting black on one side and silver on the other and made dug out shelters in the woods where they planned to hide if Hitler came. Many of them would cycle round visiting crashes and bombsites to see what they could scrounge. Some even raided the Ordnance Stores in Swinley Woods and kept cartridges and grenades under their beds.

The Ministry of Salvage encouraged the collection of all useful waste and it was the Boy Scouts who had the weekly job of collecting paper. A vigorous correspondence in the local papers reports on the extent of their activities. Mrs Philip Hill provided the local van used for the collection of salvage until 1943 when it broke down and the WRDC stepped in. They were able to pay for the new van out of the profits made from the salvage of paper and cardboard. Some of the money went to the Council and some to the Boy Scouts Fund. Another popular job for boys was to act as casualties for the girls who were Red Cross cadets. On Home Guard training days many a local lad was treated as a mustard gas victim or swathed in bandages until they were immobilised completely.

In spite of this many young men couldn't wait to join up. A good number of them joined the Air Training Corps. There were two local squadrons of the ATC, at Bracknell and Ascot. Percy Hathaway, George Laney and Arthur Clark joined the 1897 Ascot Squadron based at Dormy House in Sunningdale. Gordon Butcher belonged to the Bracknell Squadron and had his first flight in a Dominee, a civilian version of this was the Dragon Rapide. He also remembers going up in a Miles Monarch. The Bracknell squadron was based at Ranelagh Grammar School. They met every Thursday at the British Legion Hall in Cranbourne and went to Ranelagh on Sundays.

The Dormy House Sunningdale

All the local cadets trained at Woodley airfield on three Dominees, three Tiger Moths, three Oxfords, a Wellington and a Dakota. Woodley airfield belonged to the Miles Aircraft Company. They had glider lessons at Bray airfield. For all the boys this was regarded as getting ready to *"play our part"*.

"How we lived then: Digging for Victory, Rationing and Obeying the Regulations"

Never had this area been so intensively farmed as it was during the war years. All the land that could be used for agriculture including the large estates and parks was put down to the plough or for pasture. Professional gardeners, foresters and horticulturalists such as Eric Savill and Hope Finlay of the Savill Gardens and Windsor Great Park served

75

on the War Agricultural Committee set up to ensure that all land was used as productively as possible. Sir Hugh Cunliffe Owen, Chairman of the British American Tobacco Company and the owner of Sunningdale Park (now the Civil Service College), expanded his dairy herd, kept sheep and poultry and produced vegetables and soft fruit. The only larger farm in the Sunningdale area was the Home Farm at Cowarth. Golf Courses were also expected to contribute to the Food Effort. The Ministry of Agriculture determined that on the average 18 hole golf course there should be 15 to 20 acres available for agriculture *"without substantially in any way interfering with the normal use of the course"*. The Swinley Golf Course for example released some land for pasture and two acres were ploughed for barley or potatoes.

Windsor Great Park led the way in this transformation of parkland into farmland. The Royal herd of a thousand red deer and the smaller herd of Cashmere goats were culled or sent away. A hundred deer were kept as breeding stock in an enclosure up to 1948 when they were finally removed altogether. The herd was re-established in 1979/80.

In the winter of 1941 1,500 acres of the Great Park were ploughed up and the following summer they gathered in their first harvest from 330 acres of wheat, 150 acres of oats, 30 acres of barley as well as potatoes, swedes, beans and carrots. Even the Vinery near the Royal School was adapted to the war effort and tomato plants were grown under the ancient vine that was even larger than the one at Hampton Court. This wonderful plant was cut down in 1975.

"Dig for Victory" was a command obeyed at every level of society. The field next to the vicarage in Church Lane, Sunninghill was dug over, *"back breaking work"*, by the boys from Sunninghill School under the supervision of their teacher Mr Stroud. It was then divided up into allotments. *"Everyone had allotments"*. Allotments and vegetable gardens had always been important but they were even more vital in wartime. The growers were not helped by that bitter winter of 1939-40, the coldest for forty-five years.

Housewives dug up their own lawns and flowerbeds so that they could grow vegetables and keep rabbits. They collected sawdust from the sawmills along the A30 and dandelions from the hedgerows. Some also kept ducks and chickens. Eggs could be preserved for several months in isinglass and used for cooking. In December 1939 the Ministry suggested relaxing the restrictions on keeping livestock and poultry but the WRDC decided to maintain their usual regulations. Many kept poultry but fewer had pigs and goats because there was *"too much Red Tape"*. Even so there was still plenty of work for boys who collected acorns in the woods and pigswill from the neighbours carrying it off in buckets slung on their bicycles.

Instructed by the Government in September 1939, the WRDC established a Food Committee. As the war continued and the Government imposed controls over the sale of all food, petrol and fuel, it was the local government who had to enforce and administer the increasing burden of regulation. Food rationing began on January 8th 1940 and ration books were issued to everyone, allocating fixed rations in essential foodstuffs. A points system came into operation from December 1941. This gave each person sixteen (later twenty) points to use as they wished on a specific list of goods such as tinned fish or meat. There were special allowances for pregnant women, for men in heavy work and for vegetarians. Beekeepers could apply for an extra sugar allowance. The unsurprising result was a great increase in the number of beekeepers.

Food rations were continually modified as the war went on and it was in the early months of 1941 that they were at their lowest level. In 1942 a wider range of goods was put on ration including soap and canned and preserved food. More than fifty years later Mary Wood could still remember the weekly ration *"of 2 ounces of corned beef for 2d, 8 ounces of butter for 10d, a pound of margarine for 9d, 4 eggs, sugar, dried milk and dried egg powder"* and there are many other women who could still recite the rations they became so used to buying each week.

The shortage of butter seems to have been a problem for several young boys who could/would not eat margarine and it was usually their mothers who gave up their own ration. In spite of the rationing and shortages many children were perhaps better nourished than they are today. There was a serious effort to see that they had sufficient vitamins and supplements were issued to expectant mothers and young children. From 1942 imported orange juice from the USA replaced the blackcurrant extracts and the rosehip syrup and was much more palatable.

Families had to deposit their ration books at the local grocer's and butcher's shops and then, if they were good customers, they might get a share of any extras that came available such as small bottles of Camp coffee and cigarettes. Items that were not rationed but in short supply were reserved for the regulars and were kept under the counter. The war was certainly a difficult time for shopkeepers with so many forms to fill in and coupons to collect and deliver to the Food Offices. There were always shortages *"things were very difficult to get and easy to sell"*. In spite of this everyone reported that there was hardly any queuing in the local shops except for fish and chips and when some rare commodity like oranges suddenly became available. A consignment of oranges was so special that it was announced in the "Windsor, Slough and Eton Express" in 1943. The fruit was available *"from the 18th December at the rate of one pound per child's ration book and after five days any left might be sold to other members of the public, but retailers were asked to give preference to older children, invalids, hospitals and institutions"*.

The private trading of rabbits at a shilling each, chickens and extra eggs might have been called the Black Market by some but for others it was just the selling off and sharing out of what was available locally. There were always ways of finding extra rations and a lot of bartering went on. The cafés in Windsor had been allocated rations based on the numbers of their pre-war customers but, with fewer customers due to the war, they might have extra supplies to sell off secretly. The same thing happened with extra milk from the farmers.

Some men and boys had ferrets for rabbiting or went out with their guns and catapults to get pheasants and pigeons. This area had a long tradition of poaching. Local poachers were well known and were increasingly popular during the war because they always had something to trade. They went out early and late avoiding the elderly gamekeepers who had been left behind to guard the estates. There were fish to be caught in the Virginia Water ponds and even the pike made a very good meal when it had been well soaked in brine, stuffed and roasted.

Not everyone was accustomed to living off the land and for those who did not rear their own livestock and had no friends who went poaching and fishing, there was very little meat in the wartime diet. But most local people were used to this. Beef and lamb had rarely featured in the diet of the poorer villagers. *"Our main meal was usually a vegetable stew made with an Oxo cube and served with bread"*.

In 1940 the local butchers pointed out that the average amount spent per person, weekly, on meat before the war was 1s 6d and this was very much the same as the amount allowed by rationing. Rations were supplemented with plenty of apples, pears and plums grown in the gardens and allotments and by the wild brambles and crab apples. *"Everyone went out brambling"*. Most housewives bottled fruit in Kilner jars and saved up their own sugar rations to make jam and pickles. *"Everything that could be bottled was bottled from fruit to vegetables"*.

Aprilla Gilfrin and her father were lucky. Mrs Gilfrin had had cookery lessons from a French chef before the war and with only three ration books she could still make delicious soups. Gordon Butcher's family was also lucky. They didn't bother with an allotment because they had a garden in Course Road and father's friends were all shopkeepers such as butcher Harry Hall. This family and their evacuees also benefited from having eight ration books. *"We never went short"* is a popular refrain.

The Squander Bug, a demon insect that featured on government posters, would not have dared to enter the cottages in Sunninghill, Sunningdale and Ascot where the motto was already *"Waste Not, Want Not"*.

Squander Bug drawn by E. Morgan

Of course not everyone had access to an allotment or garden and, for those who really had to live on the basic ration, life could be very Spartan indeed. Natalie Paknadel remembered the troops setting up a field kitchen in the playground at Sunninghill School because *"after their main meal, served in billy cans, they had bread and **jam**, and we hadn't seen jam in a long time"*. There was one soup kitchen here run by the WVS in South Ascot. It was originally intended to help evacuated families until their ration books arrived which often took some weeks but it continued to provide meals for several years of the war. The WVS also made up boxes of food for bombed-out families and Paul Snook could remember these clearly. At the WRDC meetings there were several efforts to persuade the Council to fund canteens for the provision of communal meals but they were always voted down. There was just one canteen on the London Road at Sunningdale but that catered only for the convoys of soldiers in transit along the A30.

The 1942 Pie Scheme for Ascot, Sunninghill and Sunningdale was an effort to help rural areas that were too small to support a British Restaurant. There were British Restaurants in Windsor, Bracknell and Slough serving a limited but wholesome meal at a regulated price and without coupons. The pie scheme allowed shopkeepers and WVS offices to sell *"Telfords home-made meat pies"* without coupons. Many people remember these pies and opinions vary as to whether they were excellent or full of gristle. Perhaps the quality varied considerably.

Keeping warm was another challenge, though the low coal ration was alleviated around here because many families had access to scrap timber. Others were able to collect coke from the gas works. Many a child was sent off with the old pram to bring home the coke. A limit of four inches of bath water may have been an inconvenience for some but for the many who had no bathrooms that was not a problem. These families were used to sharing the hot water left over on washday. It was less pleasant at the Girls' Home evacuated to Englemere Wood where ten or more girls would wait in line to follow each other into the weekly bath.

Clothes were also on coupons from June 1941 and as the war went on there were increasing problems for families with growing children. Weddings were a real challenge in the era of clothes rationing. Scrap parachute silk was a much coveted material and many a bride was grateful for a pre-wedding present of coupons or settled for borrowing a dress from a friend.

Utility clothing designed to be durable and to save cloth made its appearance in September 1942. The garments had to be made from utility cloth. The numbers of buttons, the length of the skirts and the depth of the hems were all specified. There were no trimmings, no double-breasted suits and no turn-ups on trousers. Utility clothing was cheaper because it was free of purchase tax but it was still on coupons. Exchanges where no clothing coupons were necessary were set up for secondhand clothes. Mrs Fullarton James organised one of these at Beech Grove and the WVS ran regular shops along the same lines.

Shortages covered all sorts of commodities from Wellington boots, which had to be patched with cycle puncture kits, to zip fasteners, elastic and safety pins. Salvaging useful bits from old clothes became a national hobby and never were button boxes so important. Even the churches were affected by shortages and in 1946 St Michael's Parochial Church Council was appealing to the parishioners to donate enough coupons for a new verger's gown.

The churches were also affected by the paper shortage. All Church

Magazines were reduced to one page of local news but there were still several pages of Church News sent out to all the parishes from the Diocese. These included recipes, tips on making-do and a lengthy sentimental serial.

New crimes were created by all the new rules and regulations pouring out of the various ministries. It was no wonder that Tommy Handley's *"TTMA"* had a running gag about the Ministry of Aggravation. At the Ascot Court, while appearances on charges of drunkenness and theft fell by more than half, breaching the wartime regulations became the most frequent offence.

Grocers could be fined for making mistakes with their coupon collection and for infringing the new price regulations. Budgens Stores were fined £2 per item for selling dried fruit, jam, biscuits and oat flakes at excessive prices. All of these goods as well as many others had fixed prices by 1942. Harry Hall the butcher in Course Road was also fined for having too much bread in his sausages.

Misusing petrol was an even more serious offence. A few people were still allowed to run a car but they had to be very careful. The popular composer Ivor Novello was sentenced to four weeks in prison for using petrol on an unnecessary journey between London and his Sunningdale home. Councillor Nelson complained that his petrol allowance was insufficient to cover his council work. Some however managed to beat the system. Joseph Wigmore had a petrol allowance for his milk round. By a judicious choice of his route he could save two gallons a week which he sold off at half a crown a gallon.

Aprilla Gilfrin's father ran the Berystede Taxi Service and was very busy throughout the war. They had two Flying Standard 12s which covered half a million miles each. They could get a bicycle and a trunk in the boot and six soldiers inside. Aprilla remembers all the forms that had to be filled in to get the petrol required. Also that she had no time for holidays or for a social life. She began driving on September 15th 1939 when their two men drivers went off to the services and she was just eighteen years old. She had been due to take a driving test on the ninth of the month but it was cancelled. She never took a test, never had an accident and was still driving safely in 2005.

The roads were in a very bad state after the first dreadful winter of the war. It was so cold that the Thames froze over at Old Windsor and the landlord of the Bells of Ouzeley Inn was able to dine on the ice. Skaters enjoyed the ice on Englemere Pond and on the two ponds at Virginia Water. Few road repairs were made and this together with all the heavy military traffic left the local roads a mass of potholes and cracks, a challenge for motorists and a hazard for cyclists. The road through the Great Park to Windsor was also kept closed at night and was yet another reason to stay at home.

The principle form of transport was *"on one's own two feet"* though there were plenty of bicycles about. People simply did not travel unless it was absolutely necessary. Some of the school buses were still in action. The Cheapside children were taken to school in Sunninghill by bus but had to walk home. The Green Line bus service went to Staines and on to London but all the buses were packed with workers and many buses were diverted on to special routes to cover the local factories.

From Ascot and Sunningdale there was a good train service but the trains were usually full of soldiers on the move and sometimes disrupted by the London blitz. Train journeys were made more hazardous due to the darkened carriages and no station lights. Florence End remembered being locked in her carriage for her own protection by the guard at Sunningdale when taking her baby to Reading to see her parents. She always worried he might forget to unlock the door at Reading but he never did.

The main entertainment was listening to the wireless though not everybody had one. In our age of communications overload, it is hard to imagine a world where some people did not even have a radio. Radio programmes such as *"Much Binding in the Marsh"* and *"ITMA"* were followed avidly by those who did. The wireless was also important at work where *"Workers Playtime"* would brighten up the hard monotonous work of the munitions factories. Joyce Sheppard remembered singing along with *"Workers Playtime"* when she went home for lunch at Callaly. Her father tried to stop them from singing at the table but her mother said they should be allowed to sing because *"there was a war on"*. Everyone listened attentively to the News Reports. Enid Reeves asked her mother, *"What did they have on the news when there wasn't a war on?"* and was told, *"Well, there was the weather forecast"*.

Many of the witnesses stressed that in spite of everything, normal life went on. There was fun and there were even some extra amenities. Cinemas had been shut down on the outbreak of war but soon reopened albeit with the tightest blackout regulations in place. In 1939 this area had only one cinema, at Sunninghill, but wartime brought three more, one for the general public and two for the military, one for British servicemen at the Racecourse and one for the American servicemen at Sunninghill Park.

The Sunninghill Picture House about 1925

The Sunninghill cinema was known as The Picture House. It was originally called *"The Ascot and Sunninghill Picture House"* and is the Novello Theatre today. It had been founded by Captain Harry Brooke (brother of the then Rajah of Sarawak) in 1920 to provide *"wholesome amusement and instruction to all ages and classes"*. Henry Brooke's mother, Margaret, the Ranee of Sarawak, had laid the foundation stone and the actress Zena Dare had attended the ceremony. The Ranee's interest did not end there and as a talented pianist she often played at special performances. It was a very smart cinema indeed with a liveried doorman. There were 357 seats so the various classes and ages were closely packed. The gentry tended to go in the afternoon with *"carriages at 5 p.m."* leaving the evenings free for *"the working and trading classes"*.

After Captain Brooke's death in 1926, the manager Charles Searle, local historian and magistrate, bought the cinema and in 1936 Sydney Prince took over the management. By the outbreak of war they had refurbished the inside, providing toilets for the first time. During the war the programme was changed twice a week. All the performances were extremely popular and queues would form for half an hour before each performance. Ian Cooper remembered that in the 1950s the children's matinee tickets cost 4d, ice cream was 1d and sweets were 1d too, a well spent tanner i.e. sixpence which was the standard pocket money. The tickets had cost the same during the war but with no sweets or ice cream to be had.

83

Early in the war the Ministry of Defence (MOD) set up another entertainment hall for the troops billeted at the Racecourse. This was in the Grandstand Hall, a white brick building still standing at the eastern end of the racecourse buildings. Charles Cooper constructed a mobile projection room, necessary because the Grandstand Hall was also used for a variety of concerts and shows. (This projection room has ended its days as a pigeon house in Pembroke Close Sunninghill.) Some famous performers such as Arthur Askey, Tommy Trinder, Jack Hilton and Ann Sheridan came out of London to entertain the troops. These performances were not usually open to the general public. Occasionally a special performance was put on for a Fund Raising Event and then everyone was welcome.

To serve a wider audience the MOD built the Hermitage Cinema on the field where Budgens supermarket stands today. This was popular with both troops and locals. It was much bigger than the other cinemas and even had a circle upstairs. The first film shown there was Arthur Askey's *"Bandwagon"*. There were Saturday matinees for children and these attracted a large queue. The seats were a penny less than at the Sunninghill cinema. The children's matinees always included a serial and a main picture as well as cartoons.

A visit to this cinema is remembered as quite an experience. It was very cheaply built and the equipment and seats came from bombed out London cinemas. The film was projected from behind the screen, the film reels were often mixed up and the equipment used to break down. The many interruptions were always greeted with boos and missiles. The seats sometimes fell over and on one occasion the front rows became waterlogged and the Fire Brigade was called in to pump out the water. (The roof finally caved in on New Year's night in 1952 when more than six inches of snow fell between one and six in the morning.)

Nevertheless the Hermitage Cinema was so popular with its clientele that in 1941 a special meeting of the parish council was held to consider whether they should agree to the Sunday opening of all the cinemas. However very few councillors approved and neither did the various officials who were consulted. The Adjutant at the Ascot Depot in Swinley Woods thought it was unnecessary and Colonel Eggers of Silwood Park said they provided their own entertainment on Sunday evenings. Mr Prince insisted that he would not open the Sunninghill cinema because he needed one day a week off and in any case he lent his cinema to the Baptist Minister for Sunday services. Supporting Sunday openings Miss Primrose, a resident, and two other parishioners suggested that they would benefit the many refugees and evacuees since there were very few seats provided in the parish for anyone to rest on and it would give them all somewhere to go. But, with strong disapproval for Sunday opening from the head teachers and local vicars, the meeting finally decided that Sunday opening was not needed.

As well as *"the pictures"* there were dances and these were well attended in spite of the blackout. Percy Hathaway managed to get invited to the garrison dances at the Ascot Grandstand and he and his wife also remember the *"Tanner Hops"* at the Sunninghill Institute organised by Mrs Chapman with one penny of the entrance fee going to the Spitfire Fund. These were memorable for the rotten floor which made dancing an interesting experience but Mrs Chapman ran a well ordered affair and woe betide anyone who tried to take beer onto the premises. Many local marriages seem to have started with courtship at these dances. Gordon Butcher also remembered the dances at the Royal Engineers quarters in King's Ride but *"it was the Americans who got the girls"*. The dances at the American base of Sunninghill Park were closely policed and although local girls might be invited no local boys were allowed in.

A more sedate treat was taking tea at the Mascot Tea Rooms in Ascot. These were run by the Misses Baines who managed to make delicious cakes in spite of the shortages, put on Christmas parties for the local children and sold off the uneaten cakes on a Saturday afternoon at a tanner for a big bag.

Some of the old Ascot glamour still lingered. Wartime was certainly easier for those with money and society continued to dine and party. Sheila Tolhurst, an elegant divorcee, ran the Brook Club for *"gentlemen"*. She had raced a blue Riley Nine at Brooklands in 1932 and 1934 winning the Short Handicap Ladies Race. Her club had a wide clientele among the many officers and gentlemen billeted and working in the area. It originated at the Dormy House in Sunningdale and moved several times, first to Dry Arch Road in Sunningdale, then to Heronsbrook in Cheapside and later to Binfield.

The social world of the Ascot and Sunningdale ladies also continued, though it was now centred on good works, knitting circles, fundraising and teas for the troops. In May 1940 Mrs Mosenthal escorted a party around her gardens at Tittenhurst, famous for their glorious rhododendrons and azaleas. The party was in aid of the Red Cross.

Fund Raising

Even for those who were never exposed to the full horrors of the war there was no chance of forgetting the struggle that was going on. Fund raising was an important part of the war effort and there were regular savings weeks to collect money for war weapons such as the £46,000 raised locally for tanks in October 1942.

During *"Wings for Victory"* week, in May 1943, a Spitfire was put on display outside the Hermitage Cinema and there was a special film show for school children. G. Keeley of St Francis School won the second prize in the model and poster competition. There was an RAF exhibition in Cordes Hall, a parade and a day of displays at Silwood Park Convalescent Depot. As well as door-to-door collections there were boxes on all the shop counters. The Sunninghill target was to collect £25,000, enough for five Spitfires. They raised £39,542.

In July 1944 there was a *"Salute the Soldier"* week and the older schoolchildren were taken to the Hermitage Cinema to see the film *"Desert Victory"*. Again there were competitions for posters, models and dolls dressed as soldiers. There was also a military parade from Ascot through the Bog (South Ascot) to Sunninghill and around Sunningdale. A concert was held at the Hermitage Cinema and Count John McCormack, the Irish tenor who lived in South Ascot, sang there. He often sang at local charity concerts and in 1941 he entertained evacuated London mothers and their children in the Sunninghill cinema at a concert organized by the WVS. The Salute the Soldier Concert programme included the band of the King's Shropshire Regiment and Peter Gould who played Beethoven, Chopin and Brahms.

The most outstanding example of fundraising in Ascot, Sunningdale and Sunninghill was the *"Warship Week"* in March 1942. Commander Victor Crutchley, who had been awarded a V.C. for his bravery in the action at Zeebrugge, inaugurated the campaign and a banner was hung from the iron footbridge near the Sunninghill crossroads. A torpedo was displayed in the Gas Works showroom in Sunninghill. The local school children made posters and learned appropriate maritime poetry by heart. In this one week almost two million pounds were collected, averaging out at more than £200 per head for every man, woman and child. It was enough to pay for the full costs of HMS Euryalus and for its first refit. The HMS Euryalus was a Dido class cruiser of 5,450 tons. The keel had been laid in 1937 on Trafalgar Day at Chatham Dockyard and it was launched in June 1939 by the Hon. Mrs Douglas Vickers who lived at Englefield Green. It was commissioned in 1941.

The Euryalus in Sydney Harbour

Pen friends wrote to the ship's crew, one of whom was a local lad, Charles Goodchild. After the war he worked at Silwood Park as an electrician. The Captain sent back regular reports. A charity called The Friends of HMS Euryalus was established in March 1943 and collected funds to buy wool and presents for the crew. Local knitters produced balaclavas, socks, gloves, scarves and jerseys. At Christmas in 1944 and 1945 35,000 cigarettes were sent to the crew and magazines and periodicals were sent to the officers. Games such as ludo, a favourite with the sailors according to the chaplain, darts, cribbage and cards were also sent.

On the third of December 1943, The Friends of HMS Euryalus entertained the captain, some of the officers and forty members of the crew to lunch. Mrs Philip Hill who had helped to raise the very large local donation acted as hostess. Ascot schoolchildren were marched down to the station to welcome the crew but due to fog the trains were delayed and only the captain arrived in time for the children's welcome. The crew however did arrive in time for a lunch at the Berystede Hotel where all the food was paid for by the hotel. Afterwards the ship's company marched to the Picture House with the schoolchildren lining the roads. The captain presented the Friends with the tattered standard which had been flown during action against the Italian navy at the relief of Malta in 1942, and a plaque bearing the ship's crest. There was a concert followed by tea at Cordes Hall and a march back to the station. Queen Victoria's two granddaughters, the Princesses Helena Victoria and Marie Louise attended the presentation.

HMS Euryalus saw action in the Mediterranean, it was present at the first day of landings at Salerno, and later at Trondheim and in the Far East. It was a successful and fortunate ship and had no war casualties. When the ship came into Chatham in 1947 (the first time in dock since 1941), representatives from Ascot, Sunningdale and Sunninghill attended a dinner with the ship's officers and crew. A new ship's standard was handed over to the Friends. This hangs today in St Michael's Church at Sunninghill beside the old battle standard and the plaque. The Friends presented HMS Euryalus with three silver salvers, one for each of the officers' messes and a silver cup for the crew. The presentation was made by Mrs Dudley Charles, who as the local representative of the WVS, had organised many of the gifts sent to HMS Euryalus during the war. The WVS had even collected an extra £600 to buy a piano, drums and gymnastic equipment. The Friends of HMS Euryalus charity was closed down in April 1949 and the last £200 was transferred to King George VI's Fund for Sailors.

THIS PLAQUE IS PRESENTED TO
H.M.S. "EURYALUS"
TO COMMEMORATE HER
ADOPTION BY THE PEOPLE OF
SUNNINGHILL, SUNNINGDALE
AND ASCOT
DURING WARSHIP WEEK
FEBRUARY 28th MARCH 7th 1942.

The Euryalus Plaque in St. Michael's Church

THE ASCOT CAMPS

Sheep on the Racecourse and ATS in the Stables

One of the most dramatic wartime changes here came with the requisitioning of many of the larger houses and estates. The powers of requisition however extended far beyond property. John End has a collection of requisition books that were found in the woods opposite Virginia Water. Issued under the Orders for the Defence of the Realm they enabled the police, the army and any other services licensed to do so, to requisition men for labour on defence works and in emergencies. They were to bring with them their horses and carts, their harness and tarpaulins and their tools such as picks, shovels spades, axes and saws. This sort of requisitioning happened frequently early in the war when defensive positions were being prepared.

DEFENCE OF THE REALM ACT.

EMERGENCY ORDER, SY. D. 3.
for service on Horse Owners.

To Mr.......................

....

....

You are hereby ordered to at once send all your
horses, vehicles and harness to

....

All your vehicles should be loaded with..............

....

Should you have any tarpaulins or sheets, these
should accompany your vehicles.

(Sgd.),   M. L. SANT, CAPTAIN,
Chief Constable of Surrey.

DEFENCE OF THE REALM ACT.

EMERGENCY ORDER, SY. D. 6.
*to be served on able-bodied men fit to do manual
labour, who will not be employed in removal of
stock or vehicles.*

To Mr.......................

....

....

You are hereby ordered to present yourself at

....

If you are the owner of pick, shovel or wood-
cutting tools, you should bring these with you.

(Sgd.),   M. L. SANT, CAPTAIN,
Chief Constable of Surrey.

Blank Emergency Order Forms

Nationally 14.5 million acres of land, 25 million square feet of industrial and storage premises and 113,350 non-industrial properties were requisitioned by the State under the Emergency Powers Defence Act of 1939. Much of this was retained long after the war and there were constant questions in Parliament in the late 1940s and 1950s asking how much requisitioned land was still held by the government. It is very difficult to trace all the land that was requisitioned or to detect the use to which it was put because the surviving records are very patchy. (For a list of local requisitions see Appendix II.).

Private estates were required to make their contribution either by growing more crops or by being requisitioned by the War Office or other government departments. Buckhurst Park (now the property of the Jordanian Royal Family) was requisitioned early in the war and used by the Ministry of Food. Princess Lydia de Donskoi, the owner, moved with her daughter into the nearby Buckhurst Cottage. Fort Belvedere, a centre of interest during the abdication of King Edward VIII, became the offices for the Commissioners of Crown Lands, now the Crown Estate Office, who moved out of London for the duration of the war.

Natalie Paknadel remembered seeing *"a film in which one character said that a tragedy occurred and another asked in consternation: 'Don't tell me they are growing potatoes on Ascot Race Course'. We all laughed because at that time they were in fact grazing sheep"*. In fact this was nothing new for the Racecourse Authorities had long kept a small flock of sheep to keep the grass short. The shepherd was George Beasley of Course Road. The requisition of the Racecourse and the cessation of the races however was no laughing matter for the taxpayers of Ascot and Sunninghill who had to pay an extra 3d in the pound on their rates to make up for the lack of revenue.

Royal Hotel Ascot used by troops throughout the war

When war was declared most of the Ascot Racecourse was handed over to the War Office and a succession of regiments used the buildings as a transit camp. There were soldiers at the Racecourse all through the war and Colonel Jeffers of Burleigh Road was the Adjutant for all the troops stationed there. Huts and barracks were erected, zigzag trenches were dug, shelters were built and concrete blocks surmounted with tall pipes were installed across the Racecourse to prevent enemy planes or gliders landing on it.

V. Maxsted and P.Hathaway on a concrete block on the Racecourse in 1947

The Grandstand buildings were taken over in August 1939 by the Royal Artillery (RA) as a training centre for their reservists. John Mason, a soldier in the Royal Artillery, arrived at the Racecourse after a circuitous return from India via France as an instructor. He has especially fond memories of the lovely summer of 1940 because it was then that he met his future wife who had come to Ascot from London. By that time the Racecourse was the headquarters for the Mechanised Branch of the RA and their parked lorries were dispersed along local roads including St Mary's Hill. Throughout the war well-camouflaged army trucks were left in the leafy side roads all through our area.

In the spring of 1941 the Grandstand became a Main Supply Depot for the 46th Royal Engineers. A company of the 270 Pioneer Corps was also billeted here and the Royal Life Guards were installed at the Royal Ascot Hotel. Other buildings were used by the South Wales Borderers. It was a very crowded place when King George VI and Queen Elizabeth visited the troops at the Racecourse in December 1941.

Behind the pub at today's Ascot roundabout, and close to the Grandstand Hall there was a high wall banked with sand used as a shooting range. Schoolboys would creep in to look for spent bullets. On one occasion they found a pile of hand grenades and cycled off to Virginia Water to try hurling them into the Cascade. Fortunately they knew so little about these weapons that they failed to remove the pins and nothing happened. When they complained to an elder brother he was so horrified he told the police who took them back to the waterfall and made them retrieve all the grenades themselves.

In September 1944 some girls of the Auxiliary Territorial Service were ensconced in the rooms above the King's Stables and next to the Royal Apartments in the Jockey Club. Their rooms had nameplates such as *"Royal Servants"* and *"Servants in Livery"* which seemed to be very appropriate. Writing in her Memoir, entitled *"It was like this Miranda..."* Winifred Lane (then Winifred Banner) recorded her days at Ascot, remembered as one of her best postings. Winifred had been sent from Aldershot as one of six girls in an ATS Signals Unit. They were billeted together with the ATS drivers and some girls attached to the Army Ordnance Corps.

Observer Corps at Ascot Racecourse
Far right, Cecil Hiscock whose father had a sweet shop in Ascot

'It was pleasant to stroll in and out of the Royal Enclosure, it normally cost 30 shillings (£1.50) for the privilege, a useful amount of money at that time.... It's a lovely course with heath in the centre. Up to now we've been eating with hundreds of ROAC and Pioneer Corps men in one of the huge Tote buildings taken over by the army". In her diary Winifred added: *"where we work is a good thirty minutes walk from the billet. We're in a large house belonging to an estate. There's little work but tea is made every ten minutes we cook our own breakfasts, teas and suppers on duty, which makes a lot of washing up so it's more sustenance than signaling".* While Miss Banner was at Ascot there was a race meeting. She greatly enjoyed this especially since she made three shillings profit on her bets.

After three years of abstinence, Ascot Races resumed on the fifteenth of May 1943. There were nine days of racing held on Saturdays between May and October. The King and Queen attended the August Race Meeting and though there was no royal procession it was acclaimed as the return of Royal Ascot and was a great boost to morale. These Race Meetings were run under the aegis of the Jockey Club not by the Ascot Authority. Armed soldiers kept guard on the Grandstand roof. Gordon Butcher, who was a teenage police messenger at the time, recalled being up on the Racecourse tower in 1944 with the Observer Corps ready to identify any planes that might appear overhead. In spite of the wartime conditions, racing records were broken and Tommy Corie won five consecutive winners out of the eight-race programme.

At the end of the war, local families, evacuee families and refugees rushed to set up home in the empty army huts on the Racecourse. These were very desirable accommodation at a time when there was a great shortage of homes. The Hathaways' first married home was one of the brick army huts on the Grange car park, now the Ascot car park at the east end of the High Street. Irene Jones and her husband hurryied back with their baby from a tiny flat in Reading to settle in another hut nearby. Her father had moved in and kept it for them by sleeping there until they could arrive in person, so desperate was the need for a home. The ex-army huts were well equipped with bathrooms and kitchens and were much better than some of the local cottages. The Jones and the Hathaways and other squatters were allowed to stay in these huts paying rent to the WRD Council until they were relocated to council houses in South Ascot and in The Rise at Sunningdale.

Ascot West and the Internment Camp No 7

Another section of Crown Land in the Swinley Forest was also handed over to the Army. This was the area around the Ascot West station between the Swinley Road and Kings Ride. Ascot West station and sidings had been built in the 1860s to serve the brickyards that were all across this part of the forest. Most of this land and parts of Swinley Forest were taken over by the War Office who paid an annual rent to the Crown. Most of it was not returned to the Crown Commissioners until 1961.

The Royal Army Ordnance Corps installed the headquarters of its No. 2 Supply Depot in King's Ride House, on the east side of King's Ride, south of Englemere. Miles of munitions stores were concealed in the woods between Ascot and Bracknell and the old brickyard sidings around Ascot West were used to move the ordnance in and out of the open ended Nissen huts. The tracks in Swinley Woods, enjoyed by dog walkers today, were all part of this large military complex. No cars were allowed to stop on the nearby roads but local boys would break into the munitions huts on their foraging trips.

The Royal Engineers had offices nearby on the west side of Kings Ride where they produced and supplied maps to the armed services.

King's Ride House Ascot

Close to these two depots, on the east side of King's Road, there was an old First World War RAF store. This had become the winter headquarters of Bertram Mills Circus. Watching the parade of the animals from the station to their winter quarters was a feature of Ascot life in the 1930s. With the outbreak of war the animals and the circus departed and Internment Camp No 7 was set up, initially under the command of Major Shaw. The Camp occupied all the land formerly used by the circus with an additional piece on the southeast and two sections across in the Swinley Woods beside the Royal Engineers camp. One of these was used for the camp sewage works and another larger field later became a football pitch.

Internment Camp No 7 was one of several camps set up in 1940 when it was decided *"to scrutinize"* all resident German and Austrian aliens. Later Italian and other allies of the Axis powers were included. All British subjects who had shown Nazi or Fascist sympathies were also brought into the camps. All these, aliens and natives, were divided into three groups: C group were no risk, B group were of a moderate risk and A group were considered high risk. Both B and A groups were interned. Ascot was a camp for B type internees.

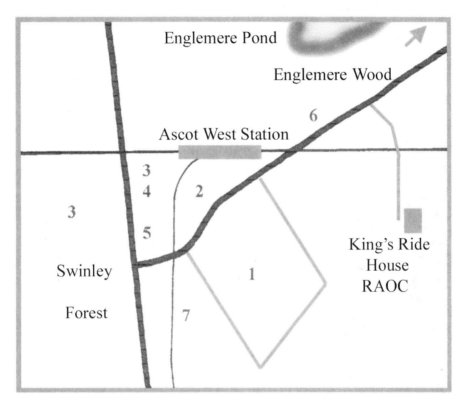

Englemere Pond

Englemere Wood

6

Ascot West Station

3

3
4
2

5

Swinley

Forest

7

1

King's Ride
House
RAOC

Ascot West Internment Camp No. 7 and Ordnance Stores
1. Internment Camp, 2. RAOC huts, offices, Sergeants' Mess & NAAFI,
3. Ordnance Stores, 4. Sewage Works, 5. Football field, 6. RE Offices,
7. Disused railway sidings.

Many of the aliens interned had fled Nazi and Fascist governments in their own countries and were of no danger to our war effort. They were naturally dismayed that the country where they had sought shelter had decided to imprison them. And even more dismayed when they found they were interned alongside British citizens who held the very anti-Jewish and fascist views from which they had fled.

At the Ascot camp there were many members of the British Union of Fascists (BUF) and other similar political parties. In his autobiography *"Blackshirts and Roses"* John Charnley, a supporter of Mosley, described the camp as *"a concentration camp at Ascot"*. He was there in 1940, when there were about seven hundred internees, three hundred more than had been expected and tents had to be used as well as hutments. They slept on palliasses stuffed with straw and there were shortages of food. The chief cook was an Austrian, a Nazi supporter who was there with his son. Some of the Italians had belonged to the Fascist Group in London. Charnley claimed that there was no antagonism between the different nationalities but he added that the Jews were ostracised and had to keep a low profile to stay out of trouble. It is clear that the combination of political prisoners with refugees made for a tense and unhappy situation.

The Compound, Ascot.
Sept. 1940.

Drawing of Internment Camp

Another fascist at the camp was George R. Merriman whose papers, lodged at the Imperial War Museum, include a list of all the Britons detained at Ascot. There is also an autograph book signed by his associates and decorated with sketches of the camp adorned with encouraging slogans such as *"Tomorrow We Live"*. Other notable fascists at Ascot were George Henry Lane Fox Pitt-Rivers, the grandson of the famous Oxford anthropologist, Frank Joyce, the brother of William Joyce (Lord Haw Haw) and the Commandant of the National Socialist

League of Camberwell in 1937, and Frank C. Wiseman, a very close ally of Mosley and a District Treasurer for the BUF.

Wiseman and eleven others were among those who wrote complaining about the conditions at No. 7 camp and demanding that they should be *"regarded as loyal subjects of the crown whatever their individual political opinions may be"*. Their complaints were listed in a Home Office Report in October 1940. The internees were particularly distressed at being forbidden to write more than two letters a week. Each letter was limited to twenty-four lines and had to be written on special paper. The paper was designed to detect the use of invisible ink and of course censorship was also the reason for the restriction on the length of the letters. They were allowed very few family visits and this was not helped by the fact that the Home Office itself did not know which internees were at Ascot and which at the camp in York. The Ascot detainees wanted freer access to their solicitors and they also wanted to know why some of them were being held for so much longer than others. They were informed that *"steps were being taken to expedite matters"*.

Twelve regional tribunals were set up to deal with appeals from the internees. These courts each consisted of three members headed by a King's Counsel. The London tribunal was often held at the Berystede Hotel, moved from London because of the bombing. Norman Birkett (later Lord Birkett) was one of the judges. Charnley was one of those who was taken to London for his hearing and he lost his appeal. Wiseman's appeal was rejected twice in 1941 and 1943. He was released in 1944 but banned from taking up his previous employment as a teacher.

Aprilla Gilfrin remembers driving one prisoner, a Dr J. Henry, from the Internment Camp to the railway station on his release. He owed her money for the fare and later sent three shillings and a letter promising to pay more when he could. He wrote that his whole life was *"in a mess after that hell of 64 days on internment without any reason"*. It seems very likely that he had been mistaken for one Dr L. V. Henry who had attended meetings of the *"Pro-British Association"*. This group was a right wing anti-Jewish organization, founded in 1940 and trying to keep alive some of the principles of the Nordic League, the National Socialist League and the British Union of Fascists after all of these had been closed down.

The internment of aliens came about as the result of press and governmental paranoia and was fostered by the fear of invasion and of a *"fifth column"* planning sabotage and terrorism. By late 1942 and early 1943 these particular fears had abated and the Ascot internees were gradually released or in a minority of cases transferred to other camps at York Racecourse, at Huyton near Liverpool and at Peel on the Isle of Man. Many of the alien internees were only released when they agreed to join the Services and a good number enlisted in the Pioneer Corps.

After 1943 the Ascot No 7 camp became a POW camp for German and Italian prisoners. They wore a navy uniform with large green patches. Richard End as an official government photographer was sent out to take all their photographs for their identity papers. Under the Geneva Convention the cells of the prisoners had to be kept artificially lit until curfew and in the winter time the locals were sure that the bright lights of the POW camp were used by German bombers as a guide on their route to London. The raiders would fly up from the south coast and turn over the camp to make their run in from the west. The German planes were also said to have used the Winkfield glasshouses as markers for their approach on the capital.

In 1944 with Italy out of the Axis Alliance, many Italian POWs were allowed to make visits outside the camp and to take on work. Schoolboys were invited to play football against an Italian team from the camp. The Italians always beat them and then entertained the lads with *"an afternoon of tea (no milk or sugar), sometimes a sandwich and games of ping-pong. The Italians always won that too"*. The POWs had decorated and painted a chapel in one of the huts and the friars from the Ascot Friary would go to conduct services for them. By July 1944, 418 Italians had left the Camp and only 174 were left there. Some were employed on local farms and market gardens.

Giovanni (John) Zerilla was one of those who moved out to another POW camp, army huts surrounded with barbed wire, set up in a field near Brockhill House Stables in Winkfield Row. He had been taken prisoner during the North African Campaign and had been in England for more than three years. He and other prisoners including some Germans were transferred to the Winkfield camp where some of them worked on the land for Wing Commander Johnson of Brock House. He settled down so well that he stayed on after the war and married Joyce Brown of Jeallots Hill. His younger brother Roberto came over from Bari in 1949. He also stayed here, married Joan Finchey and lived his life in Chavey Down Road, a stone's throw from where his wife was born.

As the Italians moved out the Germans gradually took over most of the Ascot camp. More and more of them arrived as they were taken prisoner during the liberation of Europe. Lieutenant Colonel Veitch was in command of the camp at this time. By mid-1944 the *"Ascot Experiment"* was underway, training specially selected German POWs to make propaganda broadcasts. The Camp worked in conjunction with the BBC and the American Broadcasting Authorities. Those Germans who collaborated were attacked by some of their countrymen as traitors. There were many disturbances made worse by lack of space and staff. The Camp authorities requested the removal of undesirable POWs, especially members of the Nazi party. Some were moved away and by 1945 there were only 253 Germans, Austrians and Czech prisoners left at Ascot.

During 1946, the Camp became a transit centre for the repatriation of prisoners and as many as 500 moved in and out. Some of the East Germans stayed on because they had no homes to return to. In the years after the end of the war Germans from Ascot and from the POW camp at Cobham worked at the Sunninghill Gas Works and did the groundwork for the sixty new council houses built on Brockenhurst Park in South Ascot, now known as Bouldish Farm estate. This was the first council estate to be built in the area in the 1940s. The ex-prisoners gradually found other accommodation. They made good friends here and married local girls. Three German ex-POWs joined the staff working in Windsor Great Park and were there until they retired. One of these was Walter Gimpel who lived long enough to see the reunification of Germany and to return home to live with his sister.

Army Convalescent Depot in Silwood Park

As well as requisitioning the Crown properties the two largest private estates, Silwood Park and Sunninghill Park, were taken over. Silwood Park, today part of the Imperial College of London University, was the ancient manor of Sunninghill transformed into a gentleman's park in the 1790s. Just before the war it had been acquired by the banker Sir Philip Hill. Since he lived at Sunninghill Park, Silwood Park was leased out. Carlos Clarke was the tenant in the late 1930s and the summer cricket matches played there were part of the social calendar. When war came Clarke moved out and though Sir Philip Hill continued to run the farm, the mansion and the inner park were requisitioned by the MOD and allocated to the Army.

From early in 1940 to October 1946 Silwood became the Number 118 British Army Convalescent Training Depot. There were wards, barracks, operating theatres, a gymnasium and an assault course. The site was full of Nissen huts. Local Air Cadets were also allowed to use the training facilities.

After Dunkirk it became very busy and many injured servicemen passed through its doors. Most were restored to fitness and left to rejoin their units. There were some very well known trainers including Cliff Bastin, a famous Arsenal football player. Among the PE instructors were the cricketer Denis Compton and his brother Leslie. Denis lodged at Brookside in North Ascot. His landlord was Henry Weller a cobbler in Lovel Road and a close friend of the Butcher family. Young Gordon Butcher was able to meet Denis and collect autographs which he could then sell on to his chums at Ranelagh Grammar School.

Silwood Park, Sunninghill in the late 1930s

The blue uniformed troops of Silwood Camp were well known for their attendance at St Michael's Church and they would be seen marching around the villages to improve their fitness. There were regular and very popular athletic displays put on to raise money for the war funds and their comedy shows such as the *"Convalescent Capers"* in the summer of 1941, which raised £1,400, were very well attended.

Some of the troops at the Depot had very serious injuries and their relatives would want to see them. In 1944 there were appeals in the local press and in the church magazine for people to help by accommodating relatives wishing to visit the invalids. By that date there was such a shortage of places to stay in the parish that one soldier had called in vain at ten houses to find a room for his wife. After D-Day the camp was even busier and continued in use until 1946. When it finally closed the MOD retained the Silwood Estate until 1947.

"The Yanks At The Park"

Sunninghill Park was by far the largest estate in our area. In 1939 it was owned by the banker Sir Philip Hill who had recently spent a large amount of money restoring and modernising the old house. Like Cunliffe Owen at Sunningdale Park he tried hard to avoid requisition by expanding the farming on the estate. Requisition was delayed until 1942 when the mansion, an area of 42 acres and the lake were all acquired by the Air Ministry. Farming continued on the rest of the land.

The property was handed over to the RAF who began preparing it for the arrival of the Americans. Following their entry into the war after Pearl Harbour in December 1941 there was a great need of new sites to accommodate the large forces of our new ally. All over England military camps were being established for the Americans.

The Ascot Station as the Americans called it stretched from New Mile Road to Back Lane (now Watersplash Lane). Contractors were brought in to build roads, tracks and emplacements for huts and offices and to install electricity, plumbing and telephone connections. All this activity created such a lot of mud on the roads that some Cheapside children, who had to walk home from school, were provided with Wellington boots by the Red Cross. During this work there was a fire destroying the John Flaxman reliefs in the drawing room.

The arrival of the occupants was at first very *"hush hush"*. As the Vicar wrote in the Parish magazine *"we all know who are the present tenants of Sunninghill Park but self imposed censorship is in operation"*. Nevertheless their arrival caused great excitement.

Throughout 1942 the Americans moved men and equipment to the UK. On October the first the Air Support Command of the Eighth United States Army Air Force transferred to Sunninghill Park from Membury. All the property at Sunninghill Park was officially transferred from the Air Ministry to the USAAF in June 1943. The Ninth Air Force absorbed the Eighth Air Support Command and Sunninghill became the Headquarters of the Ninth Air Force. It was here that they prepared to spearhead the invasion of the continent. Plans were being made at Sunninghill for Operation Market Garden, the Arnhem assault and for D-Day itself.

The troops at Sunninghill Park were under the command of Major General Lewis H. Brereton who had been in charge of the Ninth in North Africa and in the Far East. He had been a distinguished combat pilot in World War One and was known for having Persian carpets trimmed to fit his personal plane. Brereton commanded the first Allied Airborne Army at Nijmegen and Arnhem.

General Eisenhower became a frequent visitor. He had a house in Kingston and his Headquarters were in Grosvenor Square but he sometimes stayed at Frognal (today's Marist Convent). Sister Camilla showed me the three rooms used by Ike, two sitting rooms and a large bathroom, the latter still resplendent with its 1930s yellow suite. From the windows there was a glorious and peaceful view over parkland with a central avenue then leading to a statue of Madame du Barry, now replaced by a statue of the Madonna. Eisenhower however would have been looking across farmland rather than today's lawns because most of the Frognal estate had been ploughed up. Today the signed photograph which he presented to the nuns when he became President hangs in the entrance hall. There was at least one meeting between Eisenhower and Churchill at Charters, the post-Modernist home of the rich industrialist Frank Parkinson on the edge of Sunninghill and Sunningdale.

Locally there was a huge interest in our new friends. In the early months of 1942 and 1943 the parish magazines and the press carried articles on Roosevelt, the Episcopal Church of America and other American topics. The GIs themselves came well supplied with booklets explaining the customs of the natives and warning them of our different use of words. The information that we were short of food meant that almost every American soldier seemed to carry an endless supply of sweets, cigarettes and cookies/biscuits to the delight of the children. The whole area prospered when they arrived and there was plenty of work for everyone including the Gilfrin taxi service. Among the American officers at the camp there were some very wealthy men including Major Grey who had been the manager of the hotel "The Hollywood Bowl" and Colonel Byron C. Foy whose wife Thelma had been a Miss Chrysler. Their wives stayed at the Berystede Hotel.

One of the Americans who spent some time at Sunninghill Park was Irv Kirch who was very happy to remember his days at *"The Park"*. Irv was a radio operator in a unit that moved here from Bury St Edmunds with the 40th Mobile Communications Squadron in August 1943. The weather forecasts collected and collated from all over the United Kingdom by Irv and his mates helped to decide the all-important date of the Normandy landings.

The meteorological unit lived in tents across the lake close to New Mile Road and worked in the main house. In 2005 he wrote: *"I have many memories of my stay at Sunninghill Park some fond and some not so happy, the latter being the nightly raids by the German Air Force and having to leave a warm bed and crawling into a slit trench in the middle of the night".*

The USAAF at Sunninghill Park

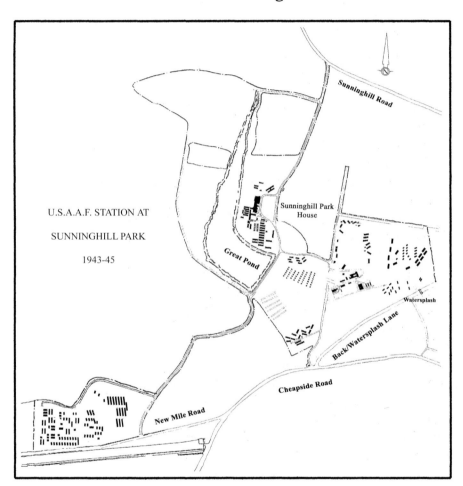

These trenches into which Irv dived whenever there were air raid warnings ran alongside New Mile Road. They were heavily sandbagged and a puzzle for the local children who thought they were a primitive form of defensive ditch. The Americans were always improving their shelters. In 1944 even as they were preparing to move out for the invasion of Europe more trenches were excavated so that there was enough space for all their troops to protect them from the VIs and V2s. Those watching were amazed to see the mechanical diggers complete such a big job in two to three days.

USAAF Personnel at The Park

Irv remembered, *"We were billeted across the lake from the large building* (this was the mansion) *that was the Headquarters for the Ninth Air Force and which contained our radio monitoring station on the top floor. I spent many a day at that building and on several occasions saw General Eisenhower coming and going. The area in which we were living was a large wooded area and I remember an English lad I would guess was about nine or ten years old, who visited us most everyday and taught yours truly how to snare rabbits on the shores of the small lake. I also remember playing baseball while we were there"*. The field where they played baseball was the Gas and Electricity Company's Field in Watersplash Lane. The Americans donated baseball equipment to the schools and established the first schoolboys' baseball league in Berkshire and Surrey.

Irv concluded: *"Some months later we built a radio shack in the woods where we lived and strung antennas from the treetops by means of a bow and arrow. It was here that me and another radio operator received the first message from members of our squadron who landed at Normandy on Dday+2"*.

Irv and his unit stayed at Sunninghill Park until late 1944.

Sunninghill Park House winter 1943-44

The USAAF Salute the Flag at Sunninghill Park

Many locals worked at the camp. Doris Woodbine was drafted to Sunninghill Park to work as a typist in 1944. She was just twenty-one years old and remembers being there on D-Day and for about three months after that. Doris worked in the Judge Advocates Office and at first they were based in huts close to New Mile Road. When the camp emptied as the Americans left for the invasion of Europe they moved into the main house. Their office dealt with all cases involving 9th USAAF service men. The offences were mostly drink or sex related or going absent without leave. The level of secrecy and protection of privacy was very high. Names and addresses of the personnel involved were always concealed.

Since Doris had been recruited by the British government she was on half the pay of most of the other typists who had been recruited directly by the USAAF and who were bussed in from Twickenham and Richmond. But Doris did share in all the perks, free lunches, nylons, sweets and cookies and the right to shop at the PX stores. She was also picked up every day from home in Bracknell and driven back.

At a time when life here was particularly drab there were many attractions in working for the Americans including Saturday dances at Sunninghill Park and at the Berkshire Golf Club that served as a USAAF Officers Mess. As well as the local girls there were a few WAAFs who acted as liaison to the RAF and some American WACs. Doris however did not go to the dances. She had her own boy friend in the RAF and had decided not to get involved with any of the Americans.

Since the war American veterans have been found in Ascot, Sunninghill and Sunningdale searching in vain for any landmarks that might take them back to *"the Park"*. One place most of them remembered well was the Thatched Tavern in Cheapside, so popular in the summer evenings. These young men far from home and unsure of their future would drink their pints on the grass opposite the pub and listen to the nightingales singing down in the valley. At the end of the night any troops who had had too much to drink or who had overstayed their time out would be rounded up by the Snowdrops, as their military police were called because of their white helmets.

It was not always so peaceful as this alas and there were fights at the Carpenters Arms in Sunninghill between the Americans and the Canadians from the Chobham camp and between the Americans and the locals. To avoid conflicts and to keep their troops in camp the USAAF provided a big entertainment centre opposite the Victorian cottages in Watersplash Lane with a wrestling ring, a cinema, a beer garden and a dance hall.

The Carpenters' Arms

The American camp quite overwhelmed the small hamlet of Cheapside nearby. Local girls worked at the camp as waitresses and cleaners. Volunteers like Mrs Greta Robinson and other ladies went to the Park to sew on buttons and repair uniforms. Local women laundered, dry-cleaned and ironed clothes. The New Inn in Sunninghill (later The Three Jays and now redeveloped as houses and flats) acted as a distribution centre. The Americans would bring in bags of washing to be handed on to women who would return it to the pub for collection and pick up their pay which might be in money but more often in goods and cigarettes. There was plenty of competition for this work.

The boys were very eager to clean shoes at a tanner a pair. *"You could make a pound in a day"* said John Wigmore. George Laney remembered going with his friends and taking their shoe cleaning kit along to the camp. They worked from five in the evening to one in the morning cleaning huge piles of boots covered in mud. They were not given money but paid in cigars and cigarettes that they sold on to their fathers and neighbours.

Some aspects of the camp were an irritation. There was a constant problem with the Parish Council over the disposal of the immense quantity of tin cans that overwhelmed the Ascot tip. The USAAF had to strengthen the roads in order to take in heavy machinery to crush the tins and there was relief when the last consignment was disposed of in January 1945. The wealth of the Americans also caused some local resentment and the GIs were not popular when one of their jeeps would draw up at the head of a queue where people were waiting to get fish and chips and the Americans would march in and buy up all the stock.

Cheapsiders were also annoyed by the daily bugle call at 7.30 a.m. and by the late evening band practices and regular gunfire. Not all the noises were unpleasant however. Some remember hearing Yehudi Menuhin playing solo violin over the Tannoy, broadcasting camp concerts across the village. More local entertainment was provided when the boxers Joe Louis and Billy Conn visited the camp and fought demonstration bouts in an open-air ring opposite the main house. Ron Tucker who ran the Boys Club took his lads along to see the boxers sparring with servicemen at The Park. Twelve year old Ginger Drew who lived in a Victorian cottage beside the camp had his photograph taken squaring up to Joe Louis. Later Ginger took part in an American broadcast telling the folks back home about the friendships between the troops and the English children.

Although some of the youngest children were scared of these big men with strange accents, their arrival was a bonanza for the local lads who sneaked into the camp over and under the fences as Irv Kirch remembered. The Woodside and Cheapside youngsters lurked around trying to scrounge what they could. This could vary from a pair of discarded shoes in the dustbins to blankets, typewriters and torches from an unguarded tent. Above all it was food they were looking for. The friendly soldiers were an endless source of all the treats that were no longer available in English shops. In spite of some petty thieving, some very good friendships were made between the boys and their American friends.

Ten-year old John Wigmore of Cheapside came to know two of the USAAF doctors very well. They let him look at blood samples through their microscope in the hospital laboratory located just inside the gate off Watersplash Lane. John knew his two friends as *"Big Doc"* and *"Little Doc"*. The latter was Doctor Keaner who was eventually invalided out. He and John stayed in touch and after Little Doc's death John continued to write to his widow Pearl. He also kept in touch with Jess Routledge (*"Big Doc"*) who came from Indiana.

Gordon Butcher remembered Lieutenant Wilmot Frank Prat, known as Chris, who became scoutmaster for the Ascot Troop when their troop leader was called up. At Christmas 1943 Gordon was allowed to invite an American to spend Christmas Day with the family and he picked Staff Sergeant Jim Blaine. Gordon lost touch with him until thirty-eight years later when he happened to buy *"The Ascot News"*. There he noticed a headline: *"American airman seeks Ascot family"* with a photograph of Jim Blaine who was trying to find the family with whom he had spent Christmas just before going off to take part in the D-Day landings. He made contact and discovered that Mr Blaine had become the administrator of the Californian Masonic Children's Home in Los Angeles. Gordon was also a Mason and they became good friends.

The Americans gave many parties for local and evacuated children. Joyce Sheppard remembered the wonderful party at the Comrades Club in 1942 with a huge Christmas tree, presents for all and the sort of food they had not seen for years. At Christmas the Americans would send jeeps to pick up the choirs from the local churches and take them along to sing carols at the Park. The choristers would then be entertained to *"wonderful teas, tinned peaches, Coca Cola and ice cream, with sweets to take home"*. Evacuated children from Kingswick were brought in to watch the movies in the camp cinema and presents were given to children who had lost their homes or parents in the war. After they had been bombed out of London Paul Snook and his family received several parcels of exciting food. At Christmas 1944 the USAAF gave a party for 600 children at the Berkshire Country Club and all the schools in the area received gifts.

By this time however most of the Americans had already left Sunninghill Park for the D-Day landings. While they were preparing to go they took their large vehicles and trucks to the weighbridge at the Gas Works. John Wigmore recalled queues of lorries all day long blocking Sunninghill High Street. Their jeeps and lorries were parked along the roadsides waiting for the action. For several days there was a continuous stream of heavy lorries and army vehicles along the A30 through Sunningdale. Louis Russell remembers being called over to a stationary vehicle where he was asked by an anxious looking soldier to post a letter for him.

Nobody spoke about all this activity because *"Careless talk cost lives"*. A special service was held secretly at St Michael's Church at three in the afternoon. The service was attended by all the American Protestant chaplains in the area and was conducted by Chaplain Walter E. Doree, a Lieutenant Colonel, assisted by Chaplain Major John F. Smeltzer. They brought their own organist and the Reverend Thursfield ensured that no one knew anything about it. The date was the 25th April 1944, only two weeks before the invasion of Europe. Even in 2005 nobody knew about this event apart from the Reverend Thursfield's daughter and a few of her close friends but it was recorded in the church papers.

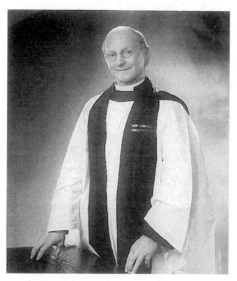

The Reverend Gerald Thursfield

In August 1944 the Ninth Air Force announced its relocation to the continent and by the fifteenth of September they had transferred from Ascot to Chantilly in France, leaving Sunninghill Park for good, an appropriate move, from one racing capital to another.

After the departure of the 9th USAAF for the battlefields of Europe, the Allied Airborne Division used some of the facilities at Sunninghill Park until several months after D-Day. Sunninghill Park was officially handed back to the Air Ministry at a ceremony on the 22nd June 1945. When the Americans finally left in the early summer of 1945 and the camp lay almost empty *"everyone descended on the Park, it was a treasure trove of food, clothing, equipment and condoms"*. They also left behind many good friends and a gap in the local community. As early as August 1944 a scrapbook was being assembled to be sent to the U.S.A. as a souvenir of the *"Americans at The Park"*. Whatever became of this book?

Some were particularly sad to see the Americans go. From 1943 onwards there had been a steady number of marriages between the GIs and local girls. Vera and Percy Hathaway recall that the first local GI bride was Doris (Dolly) Dinham of South Ascot. She married Private James Phoenix at All Souls Church on July the third 1943. All the neighbours went to her wedding. There were ten GI weddings at All Saints Ascot and nine at St Michael's Sunninghill between February 1944 and September 1945. One of the St Michael's brides was Gladys May Buckland of Pump Lane, very close to Sunninghill Park. Her marriage to Thomas B. Cooke, a USAAF Sergeant, took place in October 1945 and they left England to settle in Washington D.C. These girls were just a small part of the 40,000 GI marriages nationwide.

Gladys Buckland marries her GI

RAF Rehabilitation Camp

In the Parish Magazine of September 1945 the Reverend Thursfield welcomed 115 returning RAF POWs. Sunninghill Camp had become a Rehabilitation Camp.

Bert Melhuish had been a POW in Japan and he came to Sunninghill Park for eight months. He had had a very adventurous and difficult war. Serving in Singapore when the Japanese arrived he managed to stay with a small group from his squadron. They initially escaped capture by persuading a skipper with a river steamer to take them all to Sumatra. When Bert reached the dockside with his friend Tom, one of them was obliged to go back to collect some officers. They tossed for it and Tom lost. Bert promised to wait for him but when the skipper insisted that the boat must leave, very reluctantly Bert went on board. With the war over Bert met Tom again in Wolverhampton. *"I held out my hand to greet him after three and a half years. He did not hold out his hand but greeted me with the words, 'I thought you said you would bloody well wait for me' "*.

Bert and the rest of his squadron were eventually taken prisoner in Java and it was from there that they were taken on the *"voyage beyond belief"*, i.e. six weeks in the heat of a ship's hold to Hiroshima, where they were set to work to build ships. After the atom bombs had fallen on Hiroshima and Nagasaki, *"neither we nor Japanese knew what was happening"*, they were released and lived for several weeks on food dropped by the Americans. He then weighed six stone, half his normal weight but he was lucky to be alive at all. The survivors were taken from Japan to Sydney in Australia on the aircraft carrier *"Ruler"* where they were very well cared for by local families.

When he finally returned to England he was sent to a hospital in Wolverhampton for tests and then on to the Rehabilitation Camp at Sunninghill Park. The camp was run by Squadron Leader Boycott and housed POWs from both Germany and Japan. *"It was an easy life, there were weekly demob parties at the Canon and we were all flush with our back pay. The law even turned a blind eye when drunken ex-POWs stole cars to get home"*. Lord Nuffield gave them two motor launches to use on the lake.

They lived in the old USAAF huts and had visits from doctors and psychiatrists to help with their nightmares and other problems. There were training courses to enable them to return to normal life. Bert took a course at the Lagonda Works at Staines. During the freezing winter of 1946-1947 he tried to drive his Austin 7 across the ice of Englemere Pond but had to be dragged out by German POWs who were still at the Ascot Camp. During this incident he met his future wife Rosie Smith. His marriage led him to settle down in the area and he became the owner of the "Bracknell News".

One of the strangest stories associated with this period at Sunninghill Park concerned a canine visitor. This amazing dog called Judy was on board the gunboat *"Grasshopper"* at the fall of Singapore. She also escaped to Sumatra, was transported to Japan and survived in the POW camps where she was adopted by Leading Aircraftman Frank Williams. He managed to get her repatriated with him to England. Judy was awarded the White Cross of St Giles and in 1946 *"she paraded at the rehabilitation centres Sunnyhill (sic) Park, Ascot and Gosford wearing an embroidered coat bearing the Royal Air Force crest"*. When visiting Sunninghill Park, Judy had a special letter from the Commander giving her permission to dine with the airmen. She was *"demobbed"* in July 1946 with Frank Williams who wrote a book about her exploits.

EPILOGUE

V for Victory

During the preparations for D-Day most of the British and American soldiers vanished from Ascot. The worst of the bombing was over and in spite of the V bomb attacks everyone knew that the war would soon be over. By the spring of 1945 flags and bunting were being taken out of store cupboards and everyone was looking forward to victory celebrations. There were many parties for servicemen who had been POWs and who were now returning home. One of these was for Russell Neighbour, a sailor, who lived in Course Road at Ascot. He had been a prisoner since Dunkirk and the whole road put on a big party to welcome him home. Tragically he was killed after the war in the disaster of HMS Truculant, a submarine which sank off The Nore.

The end of the war in Europe was finally announced on May the seventh and Tuesday the eighth was declared Victory in Europe Day with a two-day holiday for all. Not everyone could believe it was really all over and of course for those with family and friends still fighting in the Far East it was not. Roma Browning was then sixteen. She remembers being told that the war was over as she was returning by train from a practice of the Girls Brigade at Ranelagh Grammar School on the Monday night. She didn't really believe it until she walked under the railway bridge and saw all the flags hanging in the streets of South Ascot.

A whole series of local services and street parties were planned to celebrate the victory. At Sunningdale there were bonfires at White's Field next to the Working Men's Club and in the Church Field in Bedford Lane, a parade through the High Street and a party in Cowarth Road that had been shut off to traffic at both ends. In South Ascot the Victory party was held in Spring Gardens and in Cheapside there was a large VE bonfire near Silwood Farm. At Sunninghill there was a bonfire on the Victory Fields followed by parties in Cordes Hall (because it was a dismally wet day) and the children were all taken to the cinema as a VE treat.

The Ascot Course Road party was a very special affair. The Americans were well known in this road because it lay across their route into Ascot and the children had made many friends with the troops. Although the main USAAF had left there was still an American presence at the Park. The Butler family had had an American billeted with them for several months. So Enid (later Reeves) who was twelve, and a friend were sent by their mothers to ask if the Americans could help with food for the party. They were taken to see the Commandant who sent them home in a jeep to the envy of their friends and they were followed by a lorry load of hamburgers, crisps, cookies, jellies and sweets.

Welcome Home Party for Russell Neighbour in Course Road, 1945

From left: Charlie Horn, evacuee at Mrs Middlemist's, Mary May, Johnnie Tidbury, Amy Beasley, Roma Tidbury, Hettie May, Enid Butler, Mrs Neighbour, Mrs R. Neighbour, Russell Neighbour, Granny Todd, Kathleen Partridge, Mrs Partridge, Mary Moss, Mr Neighbour, Mrs Moxted, Gladys Partridge, Geoffrey Law (flag), Mrs Longhurst, Richard Moss, Mrs Butler.

Enid also recalled the huge VE bonfire near the Hermitage but most of all she remembered being taken up to London for the Victory celebrations, wearing her *"Kiss-Me Quick"* hat and dancing in the crowd outside Buckingham Palace. *"It was a real thrill"* and it was the first time for many years that Ascot families had been able to visit London for pleasure.

Each parish collected funds to welcome home their service men and women. In Sunninghill the aim was to give all 275 servicemen and women ten pounds each and entertain them to a good dinner. On the tenth of June there was a large *"Welcome Home"* party on the Victory Field to raise money. The Band of the First Battalion the Royal Berkshire Regiment played to entertain the rather damp partygoers. The weather was not kind but 2,500 attended the party and Mrs Chapman organised teas for everyone. They raised £1,116 for the fund. But it was soon found that there were fifty-five more to welcome rather than the original estimate so more money had to be raised. Finally in September and October 1946, four dinners were held at the Cordes Hall and each serviceman and woman was given a cheque for six guineas which was then about a week's wages for a skilled man.

Sunningdale VE Bonfire on White's Field at Broomhall Farm

After the parties it was time to say goodbye to many of the friends and institutions that had been evacuated here. Most of the evacuees with homes to go to had already left but many others who had lost their homes in the blitz or who had settled here with their families stayed on in our parishes. The LCC schools returned to the city but the Barclay School stayed on at Little Paddocks and the Maurice Home remained at Grenville House for some years. There were still many German and Italian POWs in the area and with the division of Germany and so many displaced persons all across Europe some of these also settled here. As the servicemen came back most of the women gave up their jobs. Mary Wood lost her job as a post woman. Some of the unmarried women however went on with their work and there were scarcely any who returned to domestic service. The many volunteers who had taken on so much community work were given thanks and sometimes a gift. Miss Fullarton James who had played the organ and kept St Michael's church choir going throughout the war was presented with a *"wireless listening-in set"*.

Requisitioned property was eventually returned to its owners but very few of them returned to live in their old homes. Sir Philip Hill had died during the war and both his estates were sold off. Sunninghill Park was purchased by the Crown Estates, who thus regained an ancient Crown deer park that had been sold by King Charles I in 1630. Silwood Park was prised from the hands of the War Office and acquired by the Imperial College of the University of London as a scientific field centre.

Finally there was the question of how to remember all those who had been killed. The names of the fallen were added to the memorials erected to the victims of the First World War. The bronze plaque in St Michael's was amended by 1950 and at All Saints Ascot there was a long addition to the Roll of Honour.

Day to day life remained difficult and rationing grew even more stringent. There was exhaustion rather than a relief. Within the wartime there had been many different experiences. Those serving in the forces had widely varying wartimes depending on where they were and when they were there. Even within England, those staying at home saw the war differently according to age, sex, social position and the sheer luck of where they happened to be at some specific moment. The pervasive environment of war was however common to all, the multitude of regulations, the blackout, the rationing, gas masks, uniforms, the service men and women, the air raids and the evacuation. These had become the background to everyone's lives.

There had been a strange mixture of normality and horror. When Mary married James Wood in 1942 she had a white wedding with bridesmaids at South Ascot church. Mary made her own dress and veil and when she couldn't get white ribbon she trimmed her bouquet with the navy, gold and red ribbon from her husband's Royal Ordnance Corps. James was billeted at the Racecourse. After their marriage he was often sent into London to clear up after the blitz. Although he had been at Dunkirk he remembered his work in London as the most awful part of his war, especially terrible when he dug up the hand of a small child still clutching a penny.

Even while causing suffering, deprivation, death and injury to many, the war offered others changes of situation and opportunities that improved their lives. There might be hard grind for housewives and tough work for the men left at home but there was also excitement for young boys and new opportunities for many young women and girls. For some war brought less not more contact with others. One woman who lost her brother at the beginning of the war recalled that she really remembered very little after that. Her mother was so distressed that she spent the rest of the war years at home taking care of her.

Listening to those who still remember those years with all their problems, shortages and troubles, I heard the frequent refrain *"we really had a good war here"* followed by an expression of sadness about friends, family and acquaintances that had been lost. Of course it was those with the easier memories who were happy to talk about the war. There were some who preferred to forget all about it. There were also many whose families were broken up by the war and when looking back on their lives feel that they *"lost out because of the war"*. At the other end of the scale there are those who had found the whole war very exciting. Boys and girls too young to be in the services whose families suffered no major losses often remember the war vividly and even with pleasure. Many of the evacuees also found the experience challenging and interesting and several felt they had benefited from the experience.

None of the war memories were triumphal, but they were all regretful for the pain that had been caused even if they did not experience it directly. Many expressed a strong regret for a social cohesion that is no more. In spite of the hardness and pain they remember a time when this was still a rural area, when the villagers knew each other and when the communities were close knit. It was a period when many people were very actively working for the common good and giving their time to ease the problems caused by the war.

Some people were determined to keep the comradeship of those years going and the small hamlet of Cheapside struggled to raise money to build a community hall. They kept to their plan in spite of the disapproval of the WRDC who were not willing to back such a scheme. By December 1946 the people of Cheapside had raised the money, found and bought a piece of land and purchased an ex-army hut. This became their first community centre and since they had to manage it themselves it has kept an active community spirit going in this small hamlet.

As people struggled to reconstruct their lives and families which had been so altered, the major problem facing this corner of Berkshire was one common to most of England, a growing population and insufficient housing. The ex-army Nissen huts on the Racecourse and at Silwood Park and the Dallas huts from Sunninghill Park became homes for the evacuated families and for locals. An estate of Dallas huts was set up in Cheapside to be replaced by council houses in the 1960s.

USAAF Dallas Huts used as housing in Cheapside replaced by Hilltop Close in the 1960s.

In the post war years the whole area would change dramatically with new housing estates and developments. More and more people moved into the area. Whereas before 1939 only a few locals would travel up to London to work, these parishes now became commuter towns for the big city. The war may have brought many more people into our area as soldiers, evacuees, refugees and POWs but it was the second half of the twentieth century that saw the three villages transformed into the heavily populated areas that they are today.

Ascot, Sunningdale and Sunninghill 1939 – 1945

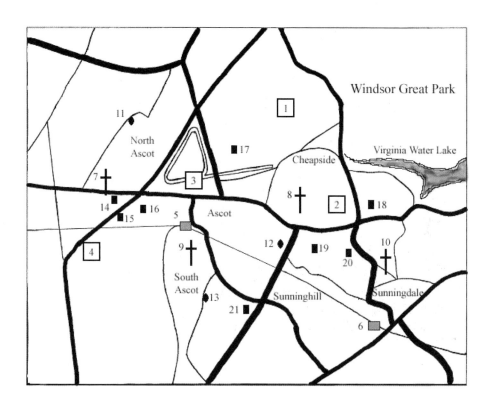

Camps

USAAF at Sunninghill Park	1
Silwood Park	2
Ascot Race Course	3
Internment Camp No 7	4

Railway Stations

Ascot	5
Sunningdale	6

Churches

All Saints, Ascot	7
St Michael's, Sunninghill	8
All Souls, South Ascot	9
Holy Trinity, Sunningdale	10

Schools

Ascot Heath	11
Sunninghill School	12
St Francis'	13

Other Buildings

Englemere Wood	14
Englemere	15
Heatherwood Hospital	16
Ascot Farm	17
Little Paddocks	18
Frognal	19
Sunningdale Park	20
Berystede Hotel	21

Appendix I

Names on Local War Memorials for 1939-1945

The following was researched by the late Philip Cooper of Sunninghill. Permission to print was given by Joan Cooper. Philip Cooper did not cover the Memorial at Sunningdale. For a photograph of this Memorial see page 9. Names in bold are not on War Memorial but in the Book of Remembrance. Names in *italics* are in the Book of Remembrance but are neither on the War Memorial nor in P. Cooper's list.

Ascot Memorial and Book of Remembrance in All Saints Ascot

Name	Age	Died	Where	Service	Buried or commemorated
Gordon F. G. Clark	23	12/01/44	Italy	L/Cpl 10th Batt. Royal Berks	Minturno War Cemetery
Ralph C. Clifford	19	16/12/43	Germany	Sgt 166 Squadron RAF	Hannover War Cemetery
Albert A. Hoptroff	22	25/05/40	France	Pte 4th Batt. Royal Berks .	Linselles
Henry B. Skyrme	23	16/01/41	England	FO 10th Squadron RAF	Runnymede Memorial
Cyril P. Matthews	20	04/12/43	England	Sgt 97th Squadron RAF	Runnymede Memorial
Roy A. F. May	22	19/11/44	Netherlands	Pte 5th Batt. Dorset. Ex R.Berks	Groesbeek Memorial
Gerald E. Merry	31	27/07/43	Italy	Sgt 12th Army Tank Regt Canadian Army	Agira War Cemetery
Ernest Openshaw	19	01/09/40	England	AB Seaman RN HMS Esk	Portsmouth Naval Memorial
William J. Openshaw	21	15/05/40	Belgium	Cpl 4th Batt. Royal Berks	Bertem
Edward G. Packer	35	29/07/45	England	Cpl Royal Army Service Corps	Clewer
Jocelyn A. Persse	29	26/10/42	Egypt	Major (Glider Pilot) Rifle Brigade	El Alamein War Cemetery
Thomas G. P. Peyton	20	28/03/42	St Nazaire	Lt Kings Royal Rifle Corps	Brookwood Memorial
Thomas B. Reay	18	17/01/41	Merchant Navy	OS Merchant Navy, SS Almeda Star	Tower Hill Memorial
Cyril E. J. Gray	21	08/11/44	India	Sgt 62 Squadron RAF	Imphal War Cemetery
V. J. W. Hawthorne	?	25/05/41	England	Petty Officer RN HMS Hood	Portsmouth Naval Mem.
William H. Helyer	21	22/02/45	Burma	Pte 2nd Batt. Royal Berks	Taukkyan War Cemetery
Thomas E. Horne	33	30/10/42	England	AB Seaman RN HMS President Doumer	Portsmouth Naval Mem.
Frederick R. A. Lewin	25	15/05/40	Norway	Lt 1st Batt. Irish Guards	Brookwood memorial
Edward C. Waite	20	10/09/43	Italy	Sapper 295 Field Coy Royal Engineers	Salerno War Cemetery

				Aircraftsman RAFVR	Ascot All Saints
Charles L. Walls	21	11/12/41	England	Aircraftsman RAFVR	Ascot All Saints
Harold A. Ward	29	14/03/44	India	Cpl 2nd Batt Leicestershires	Digboi War Cemetery
Arthur C. Austin	33	06/10/44	Italy	L/Cpl City of London Batt. R Fuseliers	Coriano War Cemetery
Herbert J. Bannister	29	24/03/45	Germany	Cpl 2-6th Airborne Div.Oxon and Bucks	Reichswald War Cemetery
William J. Bull	23	25/04/43	Tunisia	Sapper 225 Field Coy Royal Engineers	Medjez-El-Bab Mem.
Jack Butler	21	17/06/42	Egypt	Guardsman 3rd Batt. Coldstream Guards	Heliopolis War Cemetery
Geoffrey Collins	25	24/03/45	Germany	Pilot Sgt (Glider Pilot) A.A.C.	Reichswald War Cemetery
Leslie E. Cook	21	17/01/42	Algeria	PO 59 Squadron RAF	Bone War Cemetery
R. L. Cunningham	22	20/08/41	England	Lt RN HM Submarine	Portsmouth Naval Mem.
Charles N. Merry	28	12/11/42	Malaya	Pte 1st Batt. Manchester	Thanbyuzayat War Cem.
Hugh Richard Stirling	28	29/08/44	England	Major Queens Own Royal West Kent RA	Edenbridge Cemetery
Alfred J. F. Sugden	41	07/04/43	India	Lt/Col 160 Field Royal Artillery	Bhowanipore, Calcutta
Jack Taylor	21	19/05/40	Belgium	Pte 8th Infantry Royal Berks	Mere
Nigel K.W. Taylor	25	02/11/41	England	LAC RAFVR	Ascot All Saints
George W. Tolladay	29	22/04/44	Burma	Cpl 1st Batt Royal Berks	Rangoon Memorial
Victor G. Woolgar	18	05/04/46	Germany	Pte Royal Signals Corps	Hamburg
R. Mansfield				Pte Oxon/Bucks Light Infantry	
Edmund C Toy				Lieut RN Air Service	

All Souls' Ascot Memorial

Name	Age	Died	Where	Service	Buried or commemorated
John C. N. Lewis	?	02/05/43	England	FO (Pilot) RAF	Brampton
D. A Weatherill DFC	22	24/06/44	Belgium	FO (Air Gunner) RAFVR	Coxyde Military Cemetery
Georges P. O. Grove	29	31/10/42	Merchant Navy	Chf Stewd Royal London MVDalhousie	Tower Hill Memorial
H (Jumbo) O Lee	20	26/05/40	France	Pte 4th Batt Royal Berks	Gretinier
Robert Lee	32	24/06/44	Dieppe	Sgt 43rd Gloucestershire Rec. Corps	Dieppe War Cemetery
Arthur R. Perkins	21	15/06/40	Dunkirk	Pte 4th Batt Royal Berks	Sunninghill
William H. Rhodes	36	19/08/42	Dieppe	Marine RM Commando	Pihen-les-Guines
Archelaeus Turner	31	21/12/44	Italy	Pte 9th Batt Royal Fusilier	Forli War Cemetery

Harold R. Turner	22	01/01/43	England	AB Stoker RN HMS Fidelity	Portsmouth Naval Mem.
John G. E. Bradshaw	21	04/10/44	Netherlands	Pte 4th Batt Wiltshire Reg	Groesbeek Memorial
George E. V. Ryan	21	02/01/41	England	Pte 1st Batt East Surrey	All Souls Ascot

St Michael's Sunninghill Memorial

Names with * appear on the All Soul's Memorial)

Name	Age	Died	Where	Service	Buried or commemorated
Marguerite E Rance	19	09/05/42	England	AC1 WAAF	Sunninghill
Henry J. Rickens	28	17/02/43	N. Ireland	Fus 5th Batt Royal Innerskilling Fusiliers	Sunninghill
Bert Sharpe	?	22/07/43	Italy	Pte 10th Batt Royal Berks	Catania War Cemetery
Herbert Owen Lee *					
Robert Lee *					
William G(C) Morse	22	03/04/45	Germany	Pte Royal Scots/South Lancs Paras.	Reichswald War Cemetery
Arthur R Perkins *					
William Elcock	27	02/08/44	France	Pte 7th Batt Hampshires	Hottot-Les-Baques War Cem.
Ernest C George	21	24/01/45	Burma	L Cpl 9th Batt Royal Sussex	Rangoon Memorial
William A George	26	09/12/44	Italy	Driver RA Service Corps	Arezzo War Cemetery
Frederick J Hawthorn	35	27/05/44	India	Pte 1st Batt Royal Berks	Kohima War Cemetery
Jesse F Hopkins	24	14/05/44	Italy	Pte 1st Batt Queens Own R West Kents	Cassino War Cemetery
Arthur E Jupp	22	11/03/43	England	LAC 85 Squadron RAFVR	Sunninghill
Kenneth H V Keel	21	10/02/45	Germany	Pte 5th Batt Wiltshires	Reichswald War Cemetery
Hugh C Ayscough	?	13/02/40	England	Lt Col Lothian & Border Horse RAC	Sunninghill
Richard Buckland	34	15/11/43	India	Lt Royal Artillery	Kirkee War Cemetery
Terrence K Buckle	25	29/05/41	Greece	L Cpl 2nd Batt Black Watch	Athens Memorial
Frederick A Burroughs	30	25/09/40	England	AC 2 RAFVR	Staines
Jack C Chipping	28	18/07/44	France	L Cpl 3rd Royal Tank Reg. RAC	Ranville War Cemetery
Eric F Church	32	29/06/41	Merchant Navy	Fireman Trimmer SS Grayburn	Tower Hill Memorial
Terrence Draper	24	31/08/40	England	L Cpl Military Police	Sunninghill

Appendix II

Requisitions in Sunningdale, Ascot and Sunninghill

Sources: PRO, 1939 and 1945 Rate Books for WRDC in BRO and verbal reports.

Sunningdale:
From private owners:

Shrubs Hill House - *Norwegian Mission to Seamen*	War Department
Windlegate	War Department
Knolewood	War Department
Dormy House, Ridgemount Road	War Department
Cowarth Park house	War Department
Earl of Derby farmed land/US Embassy	
Auld Hame *US Army*	War Department
Callaly - *Evacuated families*	WRDC
Wisteria House - *Evacuated families*	WRDC
Dale Lodge Cottages - *Evacuated families*	WRDC
St Bruno's - *Orphanage*	Egham UDC
Heathermount *Children's home*	London CC
Horseshoe Cottage/Sunningdale Park	WRDC
Evacuated families	

Sunninghill and Ascot:
From The Crown Estate:

Ascot Hill House	War Department
Ascot Heath House and Racecourse	War Department
Car Park Holmwood	War Department
Stabling at Royal Ascot Hotel	War Department
Horse and Groom Hall	War Department
Swinley West and Forest *ROAC and RE*	War Department
Swinley Forest *Internment/POW Camp*	War Department

From private owners:

Station Hotel shed	Ministry of Food
Riding stables and loose boxes at Engelmere	War Department
Seven loose boxes in Fernbank Road	War Department
Birch Common, Brockenhurst Road	War Department
Burnside Royal Hotel, Burleigh Lane	War Department
King's Ride House	War Department
Hendersyde, Swinley Road	War Department
Hurstleigh opposite the Friary	War Department
Vaults used by SOE administrative officers	
Mylor House, New Mile Road	War Department from 1942 WRDC
Ness Woods, Monks Walk	War Department
Camp for Polish soldiers	

Silwood Park *Army Convalescent Depot*	War Department
Torwood, London Road	War Department
	later Egham UDC
Tranquillity, Swinley Road	War Department
Foreign Office used for foreign embassies	
Crossways near Frognal	Air Ministry
Oakdene, Winkfield Road	Air Ministry
Sunninghill Park - *RAF, USAAF and RAF*	Air Ministry
Daneswood *Children's home*	LCC
Ashwood, Kennel Ride - *Evacuated families*	WRDC
Ascot Lodge	WRDC
Burleigh Wood	WRDC
Clumber House, The Avenue	WRDC
Crossways London Road *Evacuated families*	WRDC
Food Control Office, Queens Road	WRDC
Little Kames, Oriental Road *Boys' Home*	WRDC
South Grange *Day Nursery*	WRDC
South Lodge, Buckhurst Park	WRDC
Udimore, Burleigh Lane *Residential Nursery*	WRDC
WVS shop in Sunninghill High Street	WRDC
Another lockup shop	WRDC

(The WRDC Sunninghill Offices were in Bowden Road during the war and were moved to Kingswick after the war.)

Property transferred privately due to War

Woodcote, Windsor Road, Ascot *from J.H. Nelson (Chairman of WRDC) to The Jewish Community*

St Michael's, Windsor Road, Ascot *to The Robert Spurrier Home for the Blind*

Little Paddocks, Sunninghill *from Horlick of Titness Park to the Barclay School*

Kingswick, Sunninghill *from Calthorpe to the LCC School for Handicapped Girls*

Kings Beeches, South Ascot *to Eversley School*

Appendix III

In January 1940, there were 1,891 evacuees in the care of the WRDC:
    1,574 school children, 125 teachers, 47 mothers, 45 nurses and helpers.

By Spring 1940 there were 1,042 persons:
    161 adults, 343 unaccompanied children, 254 families. Of these, 14 adults and 67 children were in hostels and 47 adults and 41 mothers with 115 children were in requisitioned property. The rest were billeted with families.

There was no clear collection of these statistics after this.

INDEX

INDEX